SpringerBriefs in Business

More information about this series at http://www.springer.com/series/8860

Rajendra Akerkar

Artificial Intelligence for Business

Springer

Rajendra Akerkar
Western Norway Research Institute
Sogndal, Norway

ISSN 2191-5482 ISSN 2191-5490 (electronic)
SpringerBriefs in Business
ISBN 978-3-319-97435-4 ISBN 978-3-319-97436-1 (eBook)
https://doi.org/10.1007/978-3-319-97436-1

Library of Congress Control Number: 2018950441

© The Author(s), under exclusive license to Springer International Publishing AG, part of Springer Nature 2019
This work is subject to copyright. All rights are reserved by the Publisher, whether the whole or part of the material is concerned, specifically the rights of translation, reprinting, reuse of illustrations, recitation, broadcasting, reproduction on microfilms or in any other physical way, and transmission or information storage and retrieval, electronic adaptation, computer software, or by similar or dissimilar methodology now known or hereafter developed.
The use of general descriptive names, registered names, trademarks, service marks, etc. in this publication does not imply, even in the absence of a specific statement, that such names are exempt from the relevant protective laws and regulations and therefore free for general use.
The publisher, the authors, and the editors are safe to assume that the advice and information in this book are believed to be true and accurate at the date of publication. Neither the publisher nor the authors or the editors give a warranty, express or implied, with respect to the material contained herein or for any errors or omissions that may have been made. The publisher remains neutral with regard to jurisdictional claims in published maps and institutional affiliations.

This Springer imprint is published by the registered company Springer Nature Switzerland AG
The registered company address is: Gewerbestrasse 11, 6330 Cham, Switzerland

Preface

Artificial intelligence (AI) has become a prominent business buzzword. However, many organizations continue to fail to effectively apply AI to solve specific business cases. An important characteristic of AI is that it is not static, it learns and adapts.

Artificial intelligence is the creation of "intelligent" machines – intelligent because they are taught to work, react and understand language like humans do. If you have ever used predictive search on Google, asked Siri about the weather, or requested that Alexa play your special playlist, then you have experienced AI. AI will positively and immensely change how we engage with the world around us. It is going to advance not only how business is done but the kind of work we do – and unleash new heights of creativity and inventiveness.

For businesses, the practice of AI translates straight into less time spent on routine administrative tasks internally and satisfied customers externally. Adopting AI can be cost-effective, complementary to customer engagement and useful in bridging talent gaps.

Far from merely eliminating repetitive tasks, AI should put people at the centre, augmenting the workforce by applying the capabilities of machines subsequently people can focus on higher-value analysis, decision making and innovation.

The business adoption of AI is at a very early stage but growing at a significant rate. AI is steadily passing into everyday business use. From workflow management to trend predictions and from customer service to dynamic price optimization, AI has many different usages in business. AI also offers innovative business opportunities. The AI technologies are critical in bringing about innovation, providing new business models and reshaping the way businesses operate.

This book explains in a lucid and straightforward way how AI techniques are useful in business and what we can accomplish with them. The book does not give thorough attention to all AI models and algorithms but gives an overview of the most popular and frequently used models in business.

The book is organized in six sections.

Section 1 provides a brief introduction to artificial intelligence – presents a basic concept of AI and describes its relationship with machine learning, data science and big data analytics. The section also presents other related issues.

Section 2 presents core machine learning – workflow and the most effective machine learning techniques. Machine learning is the process of teaching a computer system how to make accurate predictions when fed data. Those predictions could be answering whether a piece of fruit in a photo is a mango or an orange, spotting people crossing the road in front of a self-driving car, whether the use of the word book in a sentence relates to a paperback or a table reservation in restaurant or recognizing speech exactly to generate captions for a YouTube video.

Section 3 deals with deep learning – a common technique for developing AI applications. It is suitable for training on very large and often unstructured historical data sets of inputs and outputs. Then, specified a new input, predicting the most likely output. It is a simple intelligence method, but one which can be applied across almost every function inside a business.

Section 4 introduces recommendation engines – one of the concepts in AI has gained momentum. It is a perfect marketer tool particularly for online businesses and is very useful to increase turn around. Recommendation engine is seen as an intelligent and sophisticated salesman who knows the customer taste and style and thus can make more smart decisions about what recommendations would benefit the customer most thus increasing the possibility of a conversion. Though it started off in e-commerce, it is now gaining popularity in other sectors, including Media. The section will focus on learning to use recommendation engines for businesses to be more competitive and consumers to be more efficient.

Section 5 presents a primer on natural language processing (NLP) – a technique that gives machines the ability to read, understand and derive meaning from the human languages. Businesses are turning to NLP technology to derive understanding from the enormous amount of unstructured data available online and in call logs. The section also explores NLP for sentiment analysis focused on emotions. With the help of sentiment analysis, businesses can understand their customers better to improve their experience, which will help the businesses change their market position.

Section 6 deals with observations and insight – on employing AI solutions in business. Without finding a problem to solve, business will not gain the desired benefits when employing AI. If they are looking for a solution to detect anomalies, predict an event or outcome, or optimize a procedure or practice, then they potentially have a problem AI can address. The section begins with unfolding analytics landscape and describes how to embed AI in business processes. The section states potential business prospects of AI and the benefits that companies can realize by implementing AI in their processes.

The target audience of this informative SpringerBriefs is business students and professionals interested in AI applications in data-driven business. The book is also valuable for managers who would like to make their current processes more efficient without having to dig too deep into the technology, and executives who want to use AI to obtain a competitive advantage over their competitors.

I am grateful to many friends, colleagues and collaborators who have helped me as I have learned and taught about artificial intelligence. Particularly, I want to thank

Minsung Hong for his help in drawing figures. I thank Matthew Amboy and Springer team, who helped in book editing and production. I could not have done it without the help of these people. Finally, I must thank my family: Rupali and Shreeram for their encouragement and support.

Sogndal, Norway   Rajendra Akerkar

Contents

Introduction to Artificial Intelligence 1
Data 1
Information 2
Knowledge 2
Intelligence 3
Basic Concepts of Artificial Intelligence 3
Benefits of AI 6
Data Pyramid 6
Property of Autonomy 8
Situation Awareness 9
Business Innovation with Big Data and Artificial Intelligence 10
Overlapping of Artificial Intelligence with Other Fields 11
Ethics and Privacy Issues 13
AI and Predictive Analytics 14
Application Areas 15
Clustering or Segmentation 16
Psychographic Personas 18

Machine Learning 19
Introduction 19
Machine Learning Workflow 21
Learning Algorithms 22
    Linear Regression 22
    k-Nearest Neighbour 23
    Decision Trees 24
    Feature Construction and Data Reduction 26
    Random Forest 26
    k-Means Algorithm 26
    Dimensionality Reduction 28
    Reinforcement Learning 28
    Gradient Boosting 29
    Neural Networks 30

Deep Learning 33
Introduction.. 33
Analysing Big Data... 34
Different Deep Learning Models 36
    Autoencoders 36
    Deep Belief Net... 36
    Convolutional Neural Networks 37
    Recurrent Neural Networks 37
    Reinforcement Learning to Neural Networks......................... 38
Applications of Deep Learning in Business 38
Business Use Case Example: Deep Learning for e-Commerce 39

Recommendation Engines 41
Introduction.. 41
Recommendation System Techniques 44
    Content-Based Recommendations 44
    Collaborative Recommendations 46
    Hybrid Approaches 47
Applications of Recommendation Engines in Business 47
    Collection of Data.. 48
    Storing the Data 49
    Analysing the Data 49
Business Use Case 51

Natural Language Processing 53
Introduction.. 53
    Morphological Processing 55
    Syntax and Semantics.. 55
    Semantics and Pragmatics.. 55
Use Cases of NLP... 56
    Text Analytics 57
    Sentiment Analysis 58
Applications of NLP in Business 59
    Customer Service 59
    Reputation Monitoring 60
    Market Intelligence... 61
Sentiment Technology in Business 61

Employing AI in Business... 63
Analytics Landscape.. 63
    Application Areas... 64
    Complexity of Analytics... 64
Embedding AI into Business Processes 70
    Implementation and Action... 72

Artificial Intelligence for Growth	72
AI for Customer Service	72
Applying AI for Marketing	73
Glossary	75
References	81

Introduction to Artificial Intelligence

Data

Factual, discrete, static and dynamic things and raw observations of the given area of interest are known as data. Information can be generated after systematic processing of such data. Data are often identified as numeric values within the environment. Data can also be observed as the transactional, physical records of an enterprise's activities, which are considered as the basic building block of any information system. We require processing it before using them. Data can be defined as (Akerkar and Sajja 2010):

> Data are symbols that represent properties of objects, events and their environments. They are products of observation. To observe is to sense. The technology of sensing instrumentation is, of course, to be highly developed.

Data are the things given to the analyst, investigator, or problem-solver; they may be numbers, words, sentences, records and assumptions – just anything given, no matter what form and of what origin. This used to be well known to scholars in most fields: some wanted the word data to refer to facts, especially to instrument-readings. Others who deal with hypothesis, for them data are assumptions.

Though data is evidence to something, it need not be always true; however, there is a difficulty in "knowing" data is true or not. This leads to further processing to generate information and knowledge from available data. For example, the temperature at a particular time on given day is a singular atom of data and treated as a particular fact. There might be several such atoms, and these can be combined in various ways using the standard operations of logic. But, there are also universal statements, such as "Every day the maximum temperature is above 30 degrees". However, from logical point of view such universal statements are stronger than atoms or compounds of atoms, and thus it is more difficult to be assured about their truth. Such data are also required to be further filtered to generate necessary true information. Above all, data might be empirical data. It is very hard to assign a truth value to the fictitious non-empirical data.

Information

When data is processed, organized, structured, or presented in a given context so as to make it useful, it is called information. Though, there is information that is not data. Such distinguished information can be considered as processed data which makes decision making simpler. Processing involves an aggregation of data, calculations of data, corrections on data, etc. in such a way that it generates flow of messages. Information has normally got some meaning and purpose. That is data within a context can be considered as information.

One can add value to data in several ways:

- *Contextualized*: tells us the purpose for which the data was gathered
- *Categorized*: tells us the units of analysis or key components of the data
- *Calculated*: tells us if the data was analysed mathematically or statistically
- *Corrected*: tells us if errors have been removed from the data
- *Condensed*: tells us if the data was summarized in a more concise form

Further, information can be *processed, accessed, generated, transmitted, stored, sent, distributed, produced and consumed, searched for, used, compressed* and *duplicated*. Information can also be of diverse types with different attributes. It can be *sensitive* information, *qualitative* or *quantitative* information.

Knowledge

Knowledge is considered as human understanding of a subject matter that has been acquired through proper study and experience. Information and data may be related to a group of humans and regarded as collective mass, whereas knowledge is usually based on learning, thinking and proper understanding of the problem area by an individual. Knowledge is derived from information in the equivalent way information is derived from data. It can be considered as the synthesis and integration of human perceptive processes that helps them to draw meaningful conclusions. Knowledge is "justified true belief" related to human actions and is created from a flow of messages. Knowledge is generally personal, subjective and inherently local – it is found "within the heads of employees" rather than existing objectively.

Moreover, knowledge can be possessed outside of the human mind and suggested that *agents* are capable of manipulating beliefs and judgements. He describes knowledge as "truths and beliefs, perspectives and concepts, judgments and expectations, methodologies and know-how and is possessed by humans or other agents".

Information is the data that tells about its business and how it functions. An additional step is applied on information to convert it into knowledge, by identifying the three "I"s in the business as follows:

- Impacts: Impact of the business on the target users group and market
- Interacts: How the business system interacts with the users and other systems in the environment
- Influenced: How the business is influenced by the competitors and market trends

Within the field of knowledge management, two quite distinct and widely accepted types of knowledge exist: tacit and explicit. Tacit knowledge as identified by Polanyi is knowledge that is hard to encode and communicate. It is ephemeral and transitory and "cannot be resolved into information or itemized in the manner characteristic of information". Further, tacit knowledge is personal, context-specific and hard to formalize. On the other hand, explicit knowledge is exactly that kind of knowledge that can be encoded and is transmittable in language. It is explicit knowledge that most current knowledge management practices try to, and indeed can, capture, acquire, create, leverage, retain, codify, store, transfer and share.

Data and information are very important aspects of knowledge. It requires suitable processing to generate structured meaningful information to aid decision making and gain expertise for problem solving. That is, it is the level of processing which makes the content meaningful and applicable. By proper processing, we may generate reports which aid decision making, concepts for learning and models for problem solving.

Intelligence

Knowledge of concepts and models lead to higher level of knowledge called wisdom. One needs to apply morals, principles and expertise to gain and utilize wisdom. This takes time and requires a kind of maturity that comes with the age and experience.

The concept of wisdom has been traversed by the ancient Greek philosophers, such as Plato and Aristotle; although it has not been a popular topic of discussion in recent times. There seem to be several different strands to wisdom. A person may have encyclopaedic knowledge of the facts and figures relating to the countries of the world; but that knowledge, of itself, will not make that person wise. Instead, a person becomes wise by applying knowledge to complex problems of an ethical and practical type and looking for potential solutions.

Further enhancement on the wisdom is the intelligence. Intelligence is the aim of an entity to become full and complete artificially intelligent one.

Basic Concepts of Artificial Intelligence

Artificial intelligence (AI) has been existing through years; however, where it can be advanced is a matter of discussion. With the developing technologies, currently there is a huge demand of comprehensive human learning in computational aspects – capable of changing its own behavioural belief. Having the ability to decide, learn and inculcate itself based on the previous events and act upon it very diligently.

AI refers to manifold tools and technologies that can be combined in diverse ways to sense, cognize and perform with the ability to learn from experience and adapt over time, as illustrated in Fig. 1.

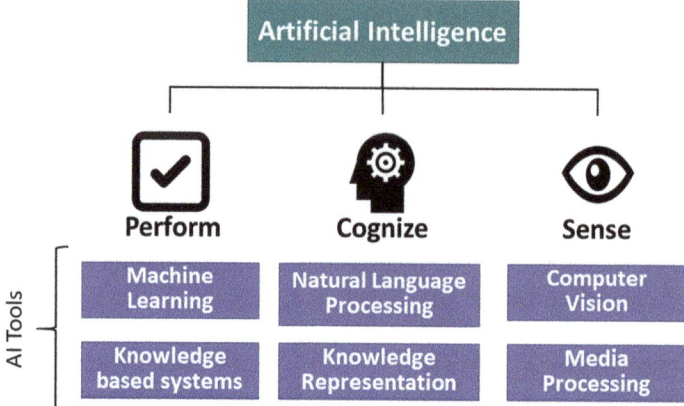

Fig. 1 what is AI?

By and large, intelligence is one's capabilities to comprehend the objective world and apply knowledge to solve problems. Intelligence of an individual consists of wide-ranging capabilities, such as: capability to perceive and understand objective things, the objective world and oneself; capability to gain experience and acquire knowledge through learning; capability to comprehend knowledge and apply knowledge and experience for problem analysis and problem solving; capabilities of association, reasoning, judgement and decision making; capability of linguistic abstraction and generalization; capabilities of discovery, invention, creativity and innovation; capability to appropriate, promptly and reasonably cope with the complex environments; and capability for predictions of and insights into the development and changes of things.

AI is not a new concept – in fact, much of its theoretical and technological underpinning was advanced over the past 62 years. For the record, AI's official start is considered the "Dartmouth conference" in 1956. And to some extent, the Turing test predates even that and offered thoughts on how to recognize an "intelligent machine". However, the journey of AI has been quite turbulent. Looking back, there has been substantial progress in almost all areas which were primarily considered to be part of AI. Let us look at some of the stimulating developments in terms of practical significance.

Knowledge-based systems were perhaps the most successful practical branch of AI. There have been several applications deployed at organizations all over the world. Hundreds of tools, commonly labelled expert system shells, were developed. Such systems achieved enough grandeur to become an independent discipline, to the extent of having separate academia courses. Along with the practical successes, the field also contributed to growth of AI itself. The concept of rule-based knowledge representation, emphasis on reasoning with uncertainty, issues of verification of domain knowledge, machine learning in the cover of automatic knowledge acquisition, etc. were some of the areas of academic growth.

Another area of progress has been natural language processing. Reasonable translation systems are available today for use in restricted context, mainly effective if a little human guidance can be provided to the system. Systran is a relevant example, which delivers real-time language solutions for internal collaboration, search, eDiscovery, content management, online customer support and e-Commerce. The field has also contributed to the development of the area of information retrieval. The World Wide Web is one of the major reasons for the interest in this area, with the available information far exceeding limits of human imagination. Without automated analysis and filtering, identifying and retrieving items of interest from this massive mine is challenging task. Semantic Web, content and link analysis of web pages, text mining, extraction of specified information from documents, automatic classification and personalized agents hunting for information of interest to a specific individual are some of the active areas today.

Speech processing has already generated functionally valuable tools. Nowadays, software tools are available which can convert your spoken text into machine processable text such as Word document. These do require some training and are not yet very effective in adapting to multiple speakers. Such tools are handy for people who do not have good typing speed, and more importantly those with disabilities to interact with computers.

Robotics is also on a high momentum path. There is a substantial Japanese initiative, which aims to develop humanoid robots to help the elderly in their routine work. This kind of initiative is currently boosting robotics work in Japan and the USA. Honda and Sony of Japan have built robots that can walk, wave, do some rudimentary dance steps, etc. Robotic pets have reached commercial status with several companies marketing sophisticated pet dogs.

What we have noted down are just a part of the successes of AI. From the modest start about half a century ago, AI has grown in many dimensions. While some of the AI practitioners are pursuing the original goal of achieving machine intelligence, bulk of AI research today is focused on solving complex practical problems.

While AI has been a part of our everyday lives for some time, this technology is at an inflection point, principally due to recent key advances in deep learning applications. Deep learning utilizes networks which are capable of unsupervised learning from data that is unstructured or unlabelled. The neural networks that underpin deep learning capabilities are becoming more efficient and accurate due to two significant recent technological advancements: an unprecedented access to big data and an increase in computing power. The effectiveness of neural networks correlates to the amount of data available.

Machine learning (ML), one of the most exciting areas of AI, involves the development of computational approaches to automatically make sense of data – this technology leverages the insight that learning is a dynamic process, made possible through examples and experiences as opposed to predefined rules. Like a human, a machine can retain information and becomes smarter over time. Contrasting a human, a machine is not inclined to sleep deprivation, distractions, information overload and short-term memory loss – that is where this influential technology becomes exciting.

With applications in almost every industry, AI promises to significantly transform existing business models while concurrently creating new ones. In financial services, for example, there are clear benefits from improved accuracy and speed in AI-optimized fraud-detection systems, forecast to be a $3B market in 2020[1].

The key advantages of AI over human intelligence are its scalability, longevity and continuous improvement capabilities. Such attributes are anticipated to vividly increase productivity, lower costs and reduce human error. Although at a promising phase, AI technology is expected to introduce a new standard for corporate productivity, competitive advantage and, ultimately, economic growth.

The enormous amount of data collected in present databases is of very limited use if only the usual retrieval mechanisms are applied. Asking the right questions and connecting the data in a way that fits to the questions may yield relevant information. A whole collection of methods is now at hand to do this, for example, data warehouses, classical statistical methods, neural networks and machine learning algorithms. AI has made a substantial contribution to data technology which is commercially used since a few years and is frequently called data mining.

Benefits of AI

- Discover meaningful and useful patterns in large volumes of data of any type, including text, images, video and other unstructured data.
- Self-learning models allow you to adapt quickly to changes in the patterns of your data and underlying business conditions.
- Make better decisions, faster by maximizing the value of all your data and moving from predictive analytics to prescriptive analytics.
- Recognize unique insights about archetypes in the data that allow optimal customer segmentation and treatments.
- Makes it easier for business users and data scientists to interpret, respond to and use data through better visualization and transparency.
- Offers new business models and value creation by accelerating innovation through the discovery of new patterns in data and fully utilizing knowledge assets.

Data Pyramid

AI systems use AI techniques, through which they achieve expert-level competence in solving problems in given areas. Such systems which use one or more experts' knowledge to solve problems in a specific domain are called *knowledge-based* or

---

[1] McKinsey Global Institute, "Artificial Intelligence the Next Digital Frontier?" (June 2017).

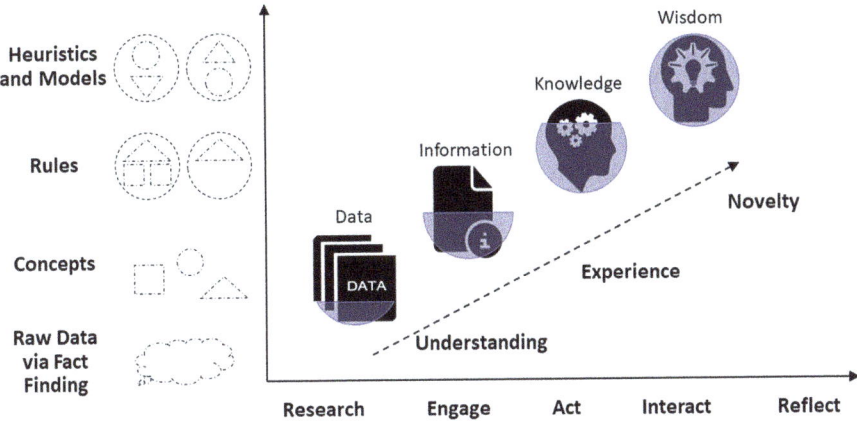

Fig. 2 Convergence from data and intelligence

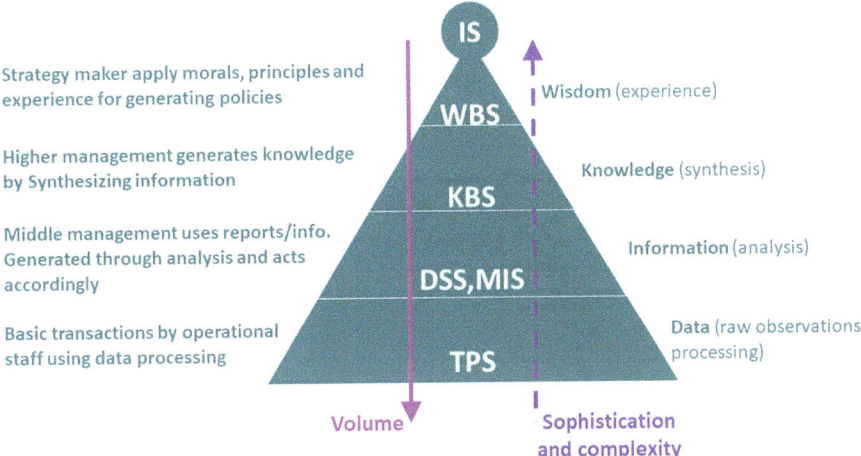

Fig. 3 Data pyramid: decision-making perspective

expert systems. Traditional information systems work on data and/or information. Figures 2 and 3 represent the data pyramid stating relations between data, information, knowledge and intelligence. Figure 2 states convergence of data to knowledge by applying activities like researching, engaging, acting, interacting and reflecting. In this process human normally gets understanding and experience and may come up with innovative ideas. These activities are shown on X-axis. Y-axis presents forms of convergence, which are namely raw observation, concepts, rules, and models and heuristics.

Figure 3 shows data pyramid through management perspectives. The operational level staff generally works with the structured environment and uses predefined procedures to carry out routine transactions of the business, which are base operations of a business. To carry out routine transaction of the business, operational staff uses system like transaction processing system (TPS). Having totally structured environment and set of predefined procedures, the development and automation of such systems (TPS) becomes easy. Such TPS considers raw observations of the field and processes them to generate meaningful information. This is the data level of the pyramid.

The information generated through the transactions of business is analysed to form routine and exceptional reports, which are helpful to the managers and executives to take decisions. The system which does this is called management information system (MIS). TPS and MIS work on structured environment working with data and/or information. The management also needs to take decision considering cost-benefit ratios of different alternative solutions available to effectively utilize the scarce resources and environmental constraints. The system category meant for that is decision support system (DSS). Unlike TPS which uses databases only and works in structured environment, the DSS normally works on structured to semi-structured environment and utilizes model base and database for optimum utilization of resources.

Systems like TPS, MIS and DSS carry out routine transactions of the business, provide detailed analysis of information generated and support decision-making process of business. However, these systems neither take decisions themselves nor justify them with proper explanations and reasoning as they do not possess knowledge. Higher level management needs knowledge and wisdom for policy and strategy making, and hence there is a need of knowledge-based and wisdom-based systems (KBS and WBS). By applying ethics, principles and judgements to the decision taken and after a level of maturity (experience), information can be generalized and converted into knowledge.

Property of Autonomy

In Computer Science distributed systems have been developed since several years and have proved to be an authoritative means for increasing efficiency of problem solving but also to open new application domains for computer technology. The contribution of AI to the field of distributed systems was not only to develop new algorithms for such systems but to equip the components of distributed systems with some degree of autonomy.

Until last decade computer systems were mostly viewed as computing machines and storages of mass data and used for decision support. Humans hesitated to accept decisions made by computer systems. However, in some technical domains computers already control big installations, which include decision making in some sense although humans still act as supervisors. Thus, computer systems have already started to become autonomous.

In multi-agent systems, which are the contribution of AI to distributedness, autonomy is a key issue. A component of a system can be viewed or modelled as an agent only if it has some degree of autonomy, otherwise it is regarded as a passive component. Autonomy can be characterized by several features. It means the capability of choosing some action from a set of possible actions in a certain situation, including the decision between staying inactive or becoming active when it is required. This ability is called proactivity.

Another important feature is the ability of maintaining goals. It is not only required that an agent can have goals that guide its planning and activity, but also that it can change them, drop them or adopt new ones. A third feature is the ability of active communication and cooperation. The word "active" is important here because the exchange of messages in the sense of functional calls between passive components usually is also called communication, but that is not meant here. Communication and cooperation between agents is also a proactive behaviour; an agent can start communication or look for cooperation with others whenever it believes it is necessary.

The property of autonomy creates a new relationship between agents – whether they are realized as robots or as software systems – and humans that has the quality of partnership. Autonomous agents can no longer be regarded as mere machines that are started when needed, do their job, and are stopped. One may view them as servants, but servants have their own will and complex cognitive abilities, and these must be conceded to the agents as well. We must expect to live in a much more complex society in the future than we do today together with agents as some kind of "living" entities. They will be present in our everyday life, for example, as personal assistants in our wearable computer system, as drivers of our car or as managers of our household. AI researchers should together with sociologists deal with the problems that may cause by this perspective.

Situation Awareness

In a general sense, all computer systems are situated, but traditional systems exist in very restricted well-defined situations completely determined by humans. Situatedness only became an important topic of research with the advent of agents in multi-agent systems and of adaptable mobile robots. Obviously, situatedness is closely related to the issue of autonomy. Only autonomous systems must locate and orientate themselves and act in situations. Situation here means a set of influences from the environment that are at least partly unforeseeable but of immense importance for the system, so that it has to react in an appropriate way.

A situated system must solve two main problems, namely how to sense the situation and how to choose an appropriate reaction. Sensing a situation may be a rather simple task for a mere software agent in a well-defined environment. However, if we think of agents acting in for example the Internet, things become much more complicated because this environment is highly unstructured and dynamic. Even more complex is sensing with robots. Here, first physical signals are to be transformed into data, a task they may delegate to physicists and engineers. But in the next step, the signals from various sources must be put together to yield a description of the situation that enables the situated system to react appropriately.

This task is called sensor fusion, and this is where AI methods come in. From Cognitive Science we learn that understanding a situation is a very complex process that requires a lot of background knowledge and a lot of nervous activity. The brain constructs the situation from the different inputs. We still know little about this process and for obvious reasons it is hard to reconstruct it. Simulations by means of AI methods may help to get insight into it. If simulation is possible, it can also be used by artificial situated systems to build up the description of a situation for their own purposes.

For situated systems the main purpose of constructing situation descriptions is to use them for their own activities. The basic tasks of self-localization and orientation and the derived task of acting can be done only based on situation descriptions. This means, on the other hand, that the construction of a situation description is always aimed to support the situated system in fulfilling its tasks, it is not an end. Criteria like completeness or consistency do not have priority, rather a description satisfies the needs of the situated system if it helps to choose the appropriate actions. Situated knowledge bases are required consisting of broad background knowledge and chunks of relevant knowledge that need not be consistent with each other nor with the background knowledge. The knowledge in these chunks may even be represented in different forms and different granularities. Methods for selecting the right knowledge chunk, for combining them, and for transforming the knowledge from one form to another must be developed.

Obviously, situated systems must have planning capabilities for choosing sequences of actions. They also must have learning capabilities because, as mentioned above, the influences that constitute a situation are partly unforeseeable. However, new situations differ not completely from each other, rather in all reasonable environments there are similarities between them, such that learning, that is, detecting and classifying similar cases, makes sense. Learning can improve the behaviour of a situated system.

Information creation, autonomy and situatedness can be regarded as focuses for the AI research and development in the future. To come up to these challenges, a lot of single methods must be integrated into greater systems. So, the general direction of AI research and development can be characterized by the development of complex systems that integrate different methods and fulfil the three requirements.

Business Innovation with Big Data and Artificial Intelligence

Demand for data has been rising over the past few years. Businesses are rushing to adopt in-house data warehouses and business analytics software and are reaching for public and private databases in search of data to spur their AI strategies. Due to the increasing demand, data is becoming a valued commodity and businesses are beginning to compete for the most lucrative reserves.

Until very recently, businesses did not realize that they were sitting on a treasure house of data and did not know what to do with it. With the innovative advances in data mining and AI, businesses can now make use of data produced by consumers and users. For example, Moz used AI to predict customer churn using a deep learning neural network that analyses user actions and can predict the behaviour of users. Since actions customers are about to perform within the system are caused by a several factors from the past, it makes it possible to mine some valuable business insights and decrease churn of existing customers, which has an enormous effect on overall company growth.

Lately, online consumer activities such as search queries, clicks or purchases were the key sources of data for large enterprises. However, as it turns out, data is plentiful in our physical environments and offline experiences as well. Big companies like Amazon have established corporate surveillance strategies in grocery stores. New sensors and actuators installed in stores can collect data about consumer preferences and behaviours. Drones, AI personal assistants and even Internet of Things (IoT) are tools that can turn every single moment of human lives into valuable data.

This data becomes a driver of price setting algorithms that reacts to changes in consumer demand. Uber has begun using this model in its price mechanism. Those businesses that stand on the edge of such innovation will have the best prospect to extract value from consumer behaviour.

One of the most promising paths is the sentiment analysis that uses NLP techniques to understand dynamics of users' emotions and feedback. With sentiment analysis, one can also identify positive and negative reviews of their products on e-commerce platforms such as Amazon. Moreover, knowing the sentiments related to your competitors can help companies assess their own performance and find ways to improve it. One benefit of sentiment analysis for managing online reputation is automation, since it can be hard to process tons of user feedback manually. Turning feedback into data to be piped into your business intelligence software is one of the most efficient solutions that will set you apart from the competition.

From chatbots and intelligent narrative generators to business analytics tools, AI is becoming a real competitive advantage for businesses that promote automation, cost reduction and intelligent decision making. However, to develop their AI strategies and train their machine learning models, businesses need high-quality data. Facebook and Google have solved this problem indeed by leveraging the user-in-the-loop model where users generate data for them via posts, comments or search queries. Some businesses gain access to data by reaching out to public and commercial databases, crowdsourcing data collection and classification services, collaborating with data-driven businesses, etc.

Whatsoever approach best fits your business model, you need to introduce effective data acquisition strategies to leverage the power of AI.

Overlapping of Artificial Intelligence with Other Fields

Artificial intelligence is the field of making machine intelligent and taking decisions with justification. This field also uses data and make machine learns. Artificial intelligence is the field which is ubiquitously applied in most of other fields and can contribute in any domain. It has an ability to learn from vast amount of data, power of simulating nature-inspired behaviour besides typical intelligent models and algorithm. This makes artificial intelligence universally applicable where typical formal model fails.

Perhaps, the most significant difference is the computational powers and the amount of data we can collect and analyse compared to previous decades. A smartphone that easily fits in a palm today can store and process more data than a mainframe computer of the 1960s, which occupied several rooms. Instead of relying on thoroughly curated and small data sets, we can use large and unorganized data with thousands of parameters to train algorithms and draw predictions. The amount and quality of data are what also differentiates modern machine learning techniques from statistics. While statistics usually rely on a few variables to capture a pattern, machine learning can be effectively utilized with thousands of data characteristics.

Machine learning is considered as an integral component of computer science and a field related to the ICT. In the field of machine learning, emphasis is given to various algorithms and techniques to make machine learn automatically from the data. Later these results are used in interpretation and application of data for problem solving. However, the field of machine learning applies some statistical and mathematical techniques.

The term *data science* was conceived back in the 1960s. As data science evolves and gains new "instruments" over time, the core business goal remains focused on finding useful patterns and yielding valuable insights from data. Today, data science is employed across a broad range of industries and aids in various analytical problems. For example, in marketing, exploring customer age, gender, location and behaviour allows for making highly targeted campaigns, evaluating how much customers are prone to make a purchase or leave. In banking, finding outlying client actions aids in detecting fraud. In healthcare, analysing patients' medical records can show the probability of having diseases, etc.

Data mining is also closely related with machine learning and AI. The term "data mining" is an inaccurate term and sounds not what it stands for. Instead of mining data itself, the discipline is about creating algorithms to extract valuable insights from large and possibly unstructured data. The basic problem of data mining is to map available data and convert it into digestible patterns. Data mining is considered to be a part of a broader process called knowledge discovery in databases (KDD) which was introduced in 1984 by Gregory Piatetsky-Shapiro. Some of the typical techniques include pattern recognition, classification, partitioning and clustering along with a few statistical models. That is, the data mining also has some overlap with statistics too.

In the era dominated by social media, customer personalization becomes one of the main sources of competitive advantages for companies offering their products and services online. Consumer analytics tools and state-of-the-art AI software for recommendation engines are the main game changers that make an efficient personalization possible in business. Data on user preferences, interests, and real-time and past behaviours can be now easily collected, stored and analysed using business analytics tools and AI algorithms. For example, insights from this data allow marketers to deliver relevant content to website visitors, video game designers to adjust the game difficulty and features to players, or recommendation engines to suggest music, videos or products that the consumers might like. Personalization powered by the data thus becomes a great tool for retaining consumers and offering them products, services and features that they are really looking for.

Ethics and Privacy Issues

Most applications of AI require enormous amount of data in order to learn and make intelligent decisions. AI is high on the agenda in most sectors due to its potential for radically improved services, commercial breakthroughs and financial gains. In the future we will face a range of legal and ethical dilemmas in the search for a balance between considerable social advances in the name of AI and fundamental privacy rights. The data and the algorithms constituting AI cannot just be accurate and high performing; they also need to satisfy privacy concerns and meet regulatory requirements. The data issues can be pronounced in heavily regulated industries such as insurance, which is shifting from a historic model based on risk pooling towards an approach that incorporates elements that predict specific risks. But some attributes are exclusive. For instance, while sex and religion factors could be used to predict some risks, they are unacceptable to regulators in some applications and jurisdictions.

As technology contests ahead of consumer expectations and preferences, businesses tread an increasingly thin line between their AI initiatives, privacy protections and customer service. For example, financial services providers are using voice-recognition technology to identify customers on the phone to save time verifying identity. Customers welcome rather than balk at this experience, in part because they value the service and trust the company not to misuse the capability or the data that enables it.

The new European Union data protection regulations that entered into force in May 2018 will strengthen our privacy rights, while intensifying the requirements made of those processing such data. Organizations will bear more responsibility for processing personal data in accordance with the regulation, and transparency requirements will be more stringent. At the same time as the requirements are being intensified, demand for data is growing. AI-based systems can become intelligent only if they have enough relevant data to learn from. An intelligent chatbot analyses all the information it is fed – a combination of questions posed by customers and responses communicated by customer service. From its analysis the chatbot can "understand" what a customer is asking about and is therefore able to give a meaningful answer. The greater the volume of information the chatbot can base its analysis on, the better and more precise will be the reply it gives.

The provisions of the General Data Protection Regulation (GDPR)[2] govern the data controller's duties and the rights of the data subject when personal information is processed. The GDPR therefore applies when artificial intelligence is under development with the help of personal data and also when it is used to analyse or reach decisions about individuals. The rules governing the processing of personal data have their basis in some fundamental principles. Article 5 of the GDPR lists the principles that apply to all personal data processing. The essence of these principles is that personal information shall be utilized in a way that protects the privacy of the data subject in the best conceivable way, and that everyone has the right to decide how his or her personal data is used. The use of personal data in the development of artificial intelligence challenges several of these principles. In summary, these principles require that personal data is:

- Processed in a lawful, fair and transparent manner (principle of legality, fairness and transparency)
- Collected for specific, expressly stated and justified purposes and not treated in a new way that is incompatible with these purposes (principle of purpose limitation)
- Adequate, relevant and limited to what is necessary for fulfilling the purposes for which it is being processed (principle of data minimization)
- Correct and, if necessary, updated (accuracy principle)
- Not stored in identifiable form for longer periods than is necessary for the purposes (principle relating to data retention periods)
- Processed in a way that ensures adequate personal data protection (principle of integrity and confidentiality)

Artificial intelligence is a rapidly developing technology. The same applies to the tools and methods that can help meet the data protection challenges posed using AI. We have collected several examples to illustrate some of the available options. These methods have not been evaluated in practice but assessed according to their possible potential. This means that technically they are perhaps unsuitable today, but the concepts are exciting, and they have the potential for further research and future use.

AI and Predictive Analytics

Predictive analytics and AI are two different things. When combined, they bring out the best in each other. AI empowers predictive analytics to be faster, smarter and more actionable than ever before. When businesses want to make data-driven predictions about future events, they rely on predictive analytics. In big data era, predictive analytics is fast becoming an important part of many businesses and functions. Predictive analytics is about using historical data to make predictions. Best example of predictive analytics is credit score. The score is based on your past

---

[2] https://www.eugdpr.org.

credit history and is used to predict how likely you are to repay your debts. While predictive analytics has been used for decades in the financial services, it is only very recently become a critical tool in other businesses. The advancement of data collection and processing technologies has made it possible to apply predictive analytics to nearly every aspect of business, from logistics to sales to human resource.

At the core of predictive analytics is the model. While the statistical techniques used to create a model depend on the specific task, they fall into two broad types. The first is the regression model, which is used to gauge the correlation between specific variables and outcomes. The resulting coefficients give you a quantified measure of that relationship, in effect, how likely a given outcome is based on a set of variables. The other type of model is the classification model. Where regression models assign a likelihood to an event, classification models predict whether rather belongs in one category or another.

Predictive modelling and analytics have been around for a while. But it has lacked three things that are important to drive real marketing value: scale, speed and application. That is where AI comes into play. With AI, predictive models can account for an incredible volume of real-time information. Such models can consider much more information than ever before, making their outputs more precise and actionable. Further, AI can evaluate billions of variables in real time and can make simultaneous decisions to analyse enormous amount of marketing opportunities per second. Without AI, a predictive model cannot make sense of that volume of data that rapidly, nor do predictive models have the "cognitive" ability to take action.

Application Areas

Customer relationship management (CRM) Using a combination of regression analysis and clustering techniques, CRM tools can separate company's customers into cohorts based on their demographics and where they are in the customer lifecycle, allowing you to target your marketing efforts in ways that are most likely to be effective.

Detecting outliers and fraud Where most predictive analytics applications look for underlying patterns, anomaly detection looks for items that stick out. Financial services have been using it to detect fraud for years, but the same statistical techniques are useful for other applications as well, including medical and pharmaceutical research.

Anticipating demand An important but challenging task for every business is predicting demand for new products and services. Earlier, these kinds of predictions were made using time-series data to make general forecasts, but now retailers are able to anonymize search data to predict sales of a given product down to the regional level.

Improving processes For manufacturers, energy producers and other businesses that rely on complex and sensitive machinery, predictive analytics can improve efficiency by anticipating what machines and parts are likely to require maintenance. Using historical performance data and real-time sensor data, these predictive models can improve performance and reduce downtime while helping to avert the kinds of major work stoppages that can occur when major systems unexpectedly fail.

Building recommendation engines Personalized recommendations are relied on by streaming services, online retailers, dating services and others to increase user loyalty and engagement. Collaborative filtering techniques use a combination of past behaviour and similarity to other users to produce recommendations, while content-based filtering assigns characteristics to items and recommends latest items based on their similarity to past items.

Improving time-to-hire and retention Businesses can use data from the human resource systems to optimize their hiring process and identify successful candidates who might be overlooked by human screeners. Also, some departments are using a mix of performance data and personality profiles to identify when employees are likely to leave or anticipate potential conflicts so that they can be proactively resolved.

Clustering or Segmentation

Clustering is the process of organizing objects into groups whose members are similar in some way. Whereas, customer segmentation is the practice of dividing a customer base into groups of individuals that are similar in specific ways relevant to marketing, such as age, gender, interests, spending habits and so on. Customer segmentation or clustering is useful in many ways. It could be used for targeted marketing. Sometimes when building predictive model, it is rather effective to cluster the data and build a separate predictive model for each cluster.

Clustering is an undirected data mining technique. This means it can be used to identify hidden patterns and structures in the data without formulating a specific hypothesis. There is no target variable in clustering. For example, the grocery retailer was not actively trying to identify fresh food lovers at the start of the analysis. It was just attempting to understand the different buying behaviours of its customer base.

Clustering is performed to identify similarities with respect to precise behaviours or dimensions. For instance, we want to identify customer segments with similar buying behaviour. Hence, clustering was performed using variables that represent the customer buying patterns.

Cluster analysis can be used to discover structures in data without providing an explanation or interpretation. Cluster analysis simply discovers patterns in data without explaining why they exist. The resulting clusters are meaningless by themselves. They need to be profiled extensively to build their identity, that is, to understand what they represent and how they are different from the parent population.

Clustering is primarily used to perform segmentation, be it customer, product or store. For example, products can be clustered together into hierarchical groups based on their attributes like use, size, brand, flavour, etc.; stores with similar characteristics – sales, size, customer base, etc. – can be clustered together.

Clustering procedure can be hierarchical where clustering is characterized by the development of a hierarchy or treelike structure.

- *Agglomerative* clustering starts with each object in a separate cluster and clusters are formed by grouping objects into bigger and bigger clusters.
- *Divisive* clustering on the other hand starts with all the objects grouped into a single cluster and clusters are then divided or split until each object is in a separate cluster.
- *K-means* clustering is a non-hierarchical clustering and is a procedure which first assigns or determines a cluster centre and then groups all the objects within a pre-specified threshold value together working out from the centre.

Deciding on the number of clusters is based on theoretical or practical considerations. In hierarchical clustering the distances at which clusters are combined can be used as criteria. In non-hierarchical clustering the ratio of the total within group variance to between group variance can be plotted against the number of clusters.

Interpreting and profiling the clusters involves examining the cluster centroids. The centroids represent the mean values of the objects contained in the cluster on each of the variables. The centroids can be assigned with a name or label. To assess reliability and validity one has to perform cluster analysis on the same data using different distance measures and compare the results to determine stability of solutions. Splitting the data randomly into halves and performing clustering separately on each half and comparing cluster centroids across two sub-samples is one of my favourite ways. In hierarchical clustering, the solution may depend on the order of cases in the data set. To achieve the best results, make multiple runs using different order of cases until the solution stabilizes.

Clustering can also be used for anomaly detection, for example, identifying fraud transactions. Cluster detection methods can be used on a sample containing only valid transactions to determine the shape and size of the "normal" cluster. When a transaction comes along that falls outside the cluster for any reason, it is suspect. This approach has been used in medicine to detect the presence of abnormal cells in tissue samples and in telecommunications to detect calling patterns indicative of fraud.

Clustering is often used to break large set of data into smaller groups that are more amenable to other techniques. For example, logistic regression results can be improved by performing it separately on smaller clusters that behave differently and may follow slightly different distributions.

In summary, clustering is a powerful technique to explore patterns structures within data and has wide applications in business analytics. There are various methods for clustering. An analyst should be familiar with multiple clustering algorithms and should be able to apply the most relevant technique as per the business needs.

Psychographic Personas

Psychographics are indicators of one's interests, behaviour, attitudes and opinions which help in understanding the reason why a persona may/may not buy a product. Psychographic data, when combined with demographic data, can give you an almost complete picture of the persona and help you choose the kind of products that can appeal to this persona.

Psychographic targeting parameters for a persona are defined by a psychological tendency for a group of people to behave in a certain manner or be attracted to similar things. So, for a young mother, the psychographic parameters would include an affinity to explore resources that give her knowledge about how to take care of her baby. On the online world, the indicators for defining the psyche of a persona would include past browsing activity, activity within website, past purchase history, claimed interests in social networking pages and other such data. Psychographic data, thus collected and pieced together, can give a very good insight as to what kind of products a persona might be interested in or capable of purchasing.

> Market segmentation is the process of separating a market into segments or groups of consumers who are similar, but different from consumers in other groups. Segmentation divides a market up into subgroups. Target marketing involves deciding which segments are most profitable. Further, positioning involves creating a product image that appeals to a target market or several target markets.

Psychographic segmentation helps construct products or position them in a way that makes them more appealing than competitors. Creating perceptual maps helps you understand how consumers see your brand and allows you to position your brand for maximum benefit. AI gathers customers into audience pools based on touchpoints and sentiment analysis, which help marketers understand how various customer segments might react to a social post, billboard or blog. By considering the way customers talk to one another, it can suggest phrases and moods that resonate best with each audience segment.

Machine Learning

Introduction

The concept of machine learning was first introduced back in the 1950s that were remarkable as the AI-pioneers time. In 1950, Alan Turing published the "Computing Machinery and Intelligence" paper that suggested a famous AI-evaluation test that we know today as Turing Test. In 1959, Arthur Lee Samuel coined the term "machine learning". Machine learning (ML) can be broadly defined as computational methods using the experience to improve the performance or to make accurate predictions. We define machine learning as a series of mathematical manipulations performed on important data in order to gain valuable insights. It is the study of algorithms that learn from examples and experience instead of hardcoded rules. Commonly, there are three main types of machine learning problems: *supervised*, *unsupervised* and *reinforcement*.

- Supervised machine learning problems are problems where we want to make predictions based on a set of examples.
- Unsupervised machine learning problems are problems where our data does not have a set of defined set of categories, but instead, we are looking for the machine learning algorithms to help us organize the data.

That means, supervised machine learning problems have a set of historical data points which we want to use to predict the future, unsupervised machine learning problems have a set of data which we are looking for machine learning to help us organize or understand.

- Reinforcement includes a specific task or goal that the system must complete. Throughout the process, it receives feedback in order to learn the desired behaviours. For example, the system encounters an error while performing the action or a reward for achieving the most favourable outcome. Thus, the program is able to learn the most effective approach via reinforcement signals.

While it seems that data mining and knowledge discovery in databases (KDD) solely address the main problem of data science, machine learning adds business efficiency to it. ML techniques can roughly be divided into four distinct areas: classification, clustering, association learning and numeric prediction. Classification applied to text is the subject of text categorization, which is the task of automatically sorting a set of documents into categories (or classes, or topics) from a predefined set. Straightforward classification of documents is employed in document indexing for information retrieval systems, text filtering (including protection from email spam), categorization of web pages and many other applications. Classification can also be used on smaller parts of text (paragraphs, sentences, words) depending on the concrete application, like document segmentation, topic tracking or word sense disambiguation. In the machine learning approach, classification algorithms (classifiers) are trained beforehand on previously sorted labelled data, before being applied to sorting unseen texts.

The use of clustering techniques with text can be achieved on two levels. Analysing collections of documents by identifying clusters of similar ones requires little more than the utilization of known clustering algorithms coupled with document similarity measures. Within document clustering can be somewhat more challenging, for it requires preprocessing text and isolating objects to cluster – sentences, words or some construct which requires derivation.

Association learning is, essentially, a generalization of classification, which aims at capturing relationships between arbitrary features (also called attributes) of examples in a data set. In this sense, classification captures only the relationships of all features to the one feature specifying the class. Straightforward application of association learning to text is not very feasible because of the high dimensionality of document representations, that is, the considerable number of features (many of which may not be very informative). Utilizing association learning on information extracted from text (using classification and/or clustering, for instance) is a different story and can yield many useful insights.

Numeric prediction (also called regression, in a wider sense of the word) is another generalization of classification, where the class feature is not discrete but continuous. This small shift in definition results in huge differences in the internals of classification and regression algorithms. However, by dividing the predicted numeric feature into a finite number of intervals, every regression algorithm can also be used for classification. The opposite is not usually possible. Again, as with association learning, simple application of regression on text is not particularly useful, except for classification (especially when a measure of belief is called for, but this can be achieved with most classification algorithms as well).

There is a difference between data mining and very popular machine learning. Still, machine learning is about creating algorithms to extract valuable insights, it is heavily focused on continuous use in dynamically changing environments and emphasizes on adjustments, retraining, and updating of algorithms based on previous experiences. The goal of machine learning is to constantly adapt to new data and discover new patterns or rules in it. Sometimes it can be realized without human guidance and explicit reprogramming.

Machine learning is the most vigorously developing field of data science today due to a number of recent theoretical and technological breakthroughs. They led to natural language processing, image recognition or even generation of new images, music and texts by machines. Machine learning remains the main "instrument" of building artificial intelligence.

To use machine learning in application or even to learn it, there are two ways. First being, learning how to use libraries that act as black box, that is, they provide different functionality. Secondly, to learn how to write algorithms and find coefficients, fit the model, find optimization points and much more so that you can curate your application as per your requirement. However, if you just want to play along, there are a few libraries and application programming interfaces that can get you your job done.

Businesses are using machine learning technology to analyse the purchase history of their customers and make personalized product recommendations for their next purchase. This ability to capture, analyse and use customer data to provide a personalized shopping experience is the future of sales and marketing.

In transport sector, based on the travel history and pattern of traveling across various routes, machine learning can help transportation companies predict potential problems that could arise on certain routes and accordingly advise their customers to opt for a different route. Transportation firms and logistics companies are gradually using machine learning technology to carry out data analysis and data modelling to make informed decisions and help their customers make smart decisions when they travel.

Machine Learning Workflow

The main difference between machine learning and traditionally programmed algorithms is the ability to process data without being explicitly programmed. This means that an engineer is not required to provide elaborate instructions to a machine on how to treat each type of data record. Instead, a machine defines these rules itself relying on input data.

Irrespective of a machine learning application, the core workflow remains the same and iteratively repeats once the results become dated or need higher accuracy. This section is focused on introducing the basic concepts that constitute the machine learning workflow as illustrated in Fig. 1.

The workflow follows the following steps:

1. *Gather data.* Use your IT infrastructure to gather as many suitable records as possible and unite them into a data set.
2. *Prepare data.* Prepare your data to be processed in the best practical way. Data preprocessing and cleaning procedures can be rather sophisticated, but generally, they aim at filling the missing values and correcting other flaws in data, like different representations of the same values in a column.

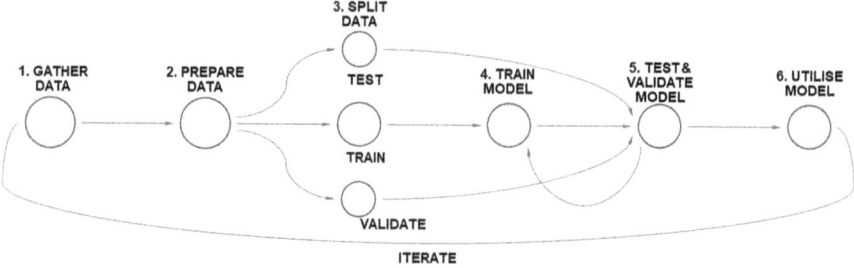

Fig. 1 Machine learning workflow

3. *Split data.* Separate subsets of data to train a model and further evaluate how it performs against new data.
4. *Train a model.* Use a subset of historic data to let the algorithm recognize the patterns in it.
5. *Test and validate a model.* Evaluate the performance of a model using testing and validation subsets of historic data and understand how accurate the prediction is.
6. *Utilize a model.* Embed the tested model into your decision-making context as a part of an analytics solution.
7. *Iterate.* Collect new data after using the model to incrementally improve it.

The essential artefact of any machine learning execution is a mathematical model, which describes how an algorithm processes new data after being trained with a subset of historic data. The goal of training is to develop a model capable of formulating a target value (attribute), some unknown value of each data object.

For example, you need to predict whether customers of your e-commerce store will make a purchase or leave. These predictions buy or leave the target attributes that we are looking for. To train a model in doing this type of predictions you "feed" an algorithm with a data set that stores different records of customer behaviours and the results, such as whether customers left or completed a purchase. By learning from this historic data, a model will be able to make predictions on future data.

Learning Algorithms

Linear Regression

A linear model uses a simple formula to find a "best fit" line through a set of data points. You find the variable you want to predict through an equation of variables you know. To find the prediction, we input the variables we know to get our answer. In other words, to find how long it will take for the cake to bake, we simply input the ingredients. There are different forms of linear model algorithms.

Linear regression, also known as "least squares regression", is the most standard form of linear model. For regression problems (the variable we are trying to predict is numerical), linear regression is the simplest linear model.

Regression algorithms are commonly used for statistical analysis and are key algorithms for use in machine learning. Regression algorithms help analysts model relationships between data points. Regression algorithms define numeric target values, instead of classes. By estimating numeric variables, these algorithms are powerful at predicting the product demand, sales figures, marketing returns, etc. For example:

- *How many items of this product will we be able to sell this year?*
- *What is going to be the travel cost for this city?*
- *What is the maximum speed for a car to sustain its operating life?*

Regression algorithms can quantify the strength of correlation between variables in a data set. In addition, regression analysis can be useful for predicting the future values of data based on historical values. However, it is important to remember regression analysis assumes that correlation relates to causation. Without understanding the context around data, regression analysis may lead you to inaccurate predictions.

Logistic regression is simply the adaptation of linear regression to classification problems (the variable we are trying to predict is a "Yes/No" answer). Logistic regression is very good for classification problems because of its shape.

Both linear regression and logistic regression have the same disadvantages. Both have the tendency to "overfit", which means the model adapts too exactly to the data at the expense of the ability to generalize to hitherto unseen data. Thus, both models are often "regularized", which means they have certain penalties to prevent overfit. Another disadvantage of linear models is that, since they are simple, they tend to have trouble predicting more complex behaviours.

k-Nearest Neighbour

k-nearest neighbour's algorithm is a method for classifying objects based on closest training examples in the feature space. It checks the feature space and can confidently give a prediction based on the nearest neighbour. It works with the fact that object that is near would have similar prediction values, and once we know the prediction value of an object, it is easy to predict for its nearest neighbour.

The *k*-nearest neighbour algorithm is one of the modest of known machine learning algorithms and it is often referred to as a lazy learner as it depends on predictions from only a specific selection of instances most like the test set instance. The training samples are described by n-dimensional numeric attributes. Each sample represents a point in an n-dimensional space; all the training samples are stored in an n-dimensional pattern space. When we have an unknown sample, the algorithm searches the pattern space for the k training samples that are closest to the unknown sample, the k training samples are the k "nearest neighbours" of the unknown sample, as shown in Fig. 2.

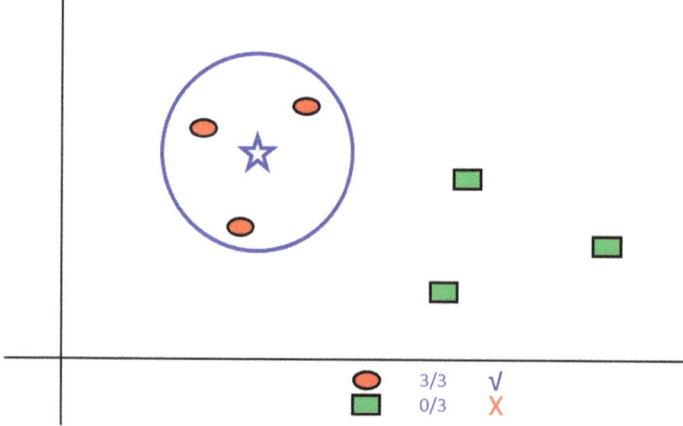

Fig. 2 *k*-nearest neighbour

k-nearest neighbour is proving to be a highly effective method for noisy training data, *k*-nearest neighbour performs well in terms of automation, as many of the algorithms are robust and give good prediction when we have data set with missing data. *k*-nearest neighbour can be improved if we have a version of decision tree to preprocess the data set. Preprocessing can be applied in several ways to our data set considering the nature of the data set; if the data set is made up of numeric attributes, the discretization algorithms would be very effective by reducing the number of tuples of the data set to much fewer intervals. The output after discretization would be fed into *k*-nearest neighbour. With this the process would be much faster since less tuples are considered.

Decision Trees

Decision tree works in the form of tree structure from the top which is referred to as the root node all the way down to the leaves; each of the branches represents outcome of the test, and the leaf nodes represent classes. To classify any unknown sample, we test the attribute of the sample against the decision tree. A path is traced from the root, that is, the top of the tree to a leaf node which holds the class prediction for that sample. Decision tree are prone to a lot of noise, and a standard technique to handling this is to prune the tree. Pruning involves removing any condition in its antecedent that does not improve the estimated accuracy of the rule. This process is meant to improve classification accuracy on unseen data.

To create or train a decision tree, we take the data that we used to train the model and find which attributes best split the train set with regards to the target. For example, a decision tree can be used in credit card fraud detection. We would find the attribute that best predicts the risk of fraud is the purchase amount (for instance, someone with the credit card has made a very large purchase). This could be the first split (or branching off) – those cards that have unusually high purchases and those that do not. Then we use the second-best attribute (e.g. that the credit card is often used) to create the next split. We can then continue until we have enough attributes to satisfy our needs.

Classification algorithms define which category the objects from the data set belong to. Thus, categories are usually related to as *classes*. By solving classification problems, you can address a variety of questions:

- *Is this email spam or not?*
- *Is this transaction duplicitous or not?*
- *Which type of product is this shopper more likely to buy: a sofa, a dining table, or garden chairs?*

Scalability is a significant issue with decision tree as it does not scale well on large data sets, and in data mining, typical training sets run into millions of samples. The scalability issue arises since training sets are kept in main memory. This restriction limits the scalability of such algorithms, where the decision tree construction can become inefficient due to swapping of the training samples in and out of main and cache memories. An option is to discretize the continuous attributes and doing our sampling at each node. But this also has its own inefficiencies. Another option is to partition large decision tree into subsets and build a decision tree from the subsets. Since we are only working on subsets, the accuracy of our result is not as good as if we used all the data set.

A set back to decision tree is the greedy nature of the algorithm. The greedy nature means that the algorithm makes commitments to certain choices too early which prevent them from finding the best overall solution later. Decision trees are very fast and classification accuracy is naturally high for data where the mapping of classes consists of long and thin regions in concept space.

An improvement to this learning technique could be to modify the algorithm to handle continuous-valued attributes. Decision tree has the attribute of being robust with respect to many predictor types. It makes it well suited as a good preprocessing method for other algorithms. An example is to preprocess data for neural networks; due to its speed it would conveniently do a first pass on the data that would create a subset of predictors which would be fed into a neural network or k-nearest neighbour. This would definitely reduce the noise content neural network has to deal with, and this would definitely improve the performance of neural network.

Another very precise classification task is *anomaly detection*. It is typically recognized as the one-class classification because the goal of anomaly detection is to find *outliers*, unusual objects in data that do not appear in its normal distribution. What kind of problems it can solve:

- *Are there any shoppers with distinctive qualities in our data set?*
- *Can we spot unusual behaviours among our insurance customers?*

Feature Construction and Data Reduction

The role of representation has been recognized as a crucial issue in AI and ML. In the paradigm of learning from examples and attribute-value representation of input data, the original representation is a vector of attributes (features, variables) describing examples (instances, objects). The transformation process of input attributes, used in feature construction, can be formulated as follows: given the original vector of features and the training set, construct a derived representation that is better given some criteria (i.e. predictive accuracy, size of representation). The new transformed attributes either replace the original attributes or can be added to the description of the examples. Examples of attribute transformations are counting, grouping, interval construction/discretization, scaling, flattening, normalization (of numerical values), clustering, principal component analysis, etc. Many transformations are possible, by applying all kinds of mathematical formulas, but in practice, only a limited number of transformations are effective.

Random Forest

A random forest is the average of several decision trees, each of which is trained with a random sample of the data. Each single tree in the forest is weaker than a full decision tree, but by putting them all together, we get better overall performance thanks to diversity.

Random forest is a very prevalent algorithm in machine learning today. It is very easy to train, and it tends to perform well. Its disadvantage is that it can be slow to output predictions relative to other algorithms, so you might not use it when you need lightning-fast predictions. Random forest gives much more accurate predictions when compared to regression models in many scenarios. These cases generally have high number of predictive variables and huge sample size. This is because it captures the variance of several input variables at the same time and enables high number of observations to participate in the prediction.

k-Means Algorithm

k-means is a type of unsupervised algorithm which solves the clustering problem. The main difference between regular classification and clustering is that the algorithm is challenged to group items in clusters without predefined classes. That means, it should decide the principles of the division itself without human guidance. Cluster analysis is typically realized within the unsupervised learning style. Clustering can solve the following problems:

- *What are the main segments of customers we have considering their demographics and behaviours?*

Fig. 3 Three clusters

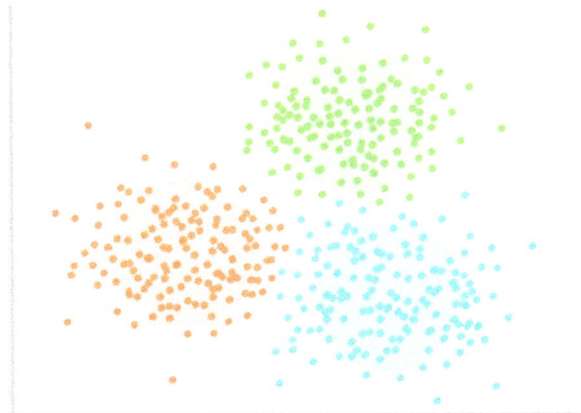

- *Is there any relationship between default risks of some bank clients and their behaviours?*
- *How can we classify the keywords that people use to reach our website?*

Its procedure follows a simple and straightforward way to classify a given data set through a certain number of clusters (assume k clusters), see Fig. 3. Data points inside a cluster are homogeneous and heterogeneous to peer groups.

How k-means forms cluster:

1. k-means picks k number of points for each cluster known as centroids.
2. Each data point forms a cluster with the closest centroids, that is, k clusters.
3. Finds the centroid of each cluster based on existing cluster members. Here we have new centroids.
4. As we have new centroids, repeat step 2 and 3. Find the closest distance for each data point from new centroids and get associated with new k-clusters. Repeat this process until convergence occurs, that is, centroids do not change.

In k-means, we have clusters and each cluster has its own centroid. Sum of square of difference between centroid and the data points within a cluster constitutes within sum of square value for that cluster. Also, when the sums of square values for all the clusters are added, it becomes total within sum of square value for the cluster solution.

We know that as the number of cluster increases, this value keeps on decreasing but if you plot the result you may see that the sum of squared distance decreases sharply up to some value of k, and then much more slowly after that. Here, we can find the optimum number of cluster.

Dimensionality Reduction

Dimensionality reduction helps systems remove data that is not useful for analysis. This group of algorithms is used to remove redundant data, outliers and other non-useful data. Dimensionality reduction can be helpful when analysing data from sensors and other Internet of Things (IoT) use cases. In IoT systems, there might be thousands of data points simply telling you that a sensor is turned on. Storing and analysing that "on" data is not helpful and will occupy important storage space. In addition, by removing this redundant data, the performance of a machine learning system will improve. Finally, dimensionality reduction will also help analysts visualize the data.

Reinforcement Learning

Reinforcement learning is a computational approach to understanding and automating goal-directed learning and decision making. It is learning what to do and how to map situations to actions. The outcome is to maximize the numerical reward signal. The learner is not told which action to take, but instead must discover which action will yield the maximum reward.

Reinforcement learning is defined not by characterizing learning algorithms, but by characterizing a learning problem. Any algorithm that is well suited to solving that problem we consider to be a reinforcement learning algorithm. Reinforcement learning is different from supervised learning, the kind of learning studied.

Supervised learning is learning from examples provided by some knowledgeable external supervisor. This is an important kind of learning, but alone it is not adequate for learning from interaction. In interactive problems, it is often impractical to obtain examples of desired behaviour that are both correct and representative of all the situations in which the agent has to act. In uncharted territory – where one would expect learning to be most beneficial – an agent must be able to learn from its own experience.

One of the challenges that arise in reinforcement learning and not in other kinds of learning is the trade-off between exploration and exploitation. To obtain a lot of reward, a reinforcement learning agent must prefer actions that it has tried in the past and found to be effective in producing reward. But to discover such actions it must try actions that it has not selected before. The agent must exploit what it already knows in order to obtain reward, but it also has to explore in order to make better action selections in the future.

The dilemma is that neither exploitation nor exploration can be pursued exclusively without failing at the task. The agent must try a variety of actions and progressively favour those that appear to be best. On a stochastic task, each action must be tried many times to reliably estimate its expected reward. The exploration–exploitation dilemma has been intensively studied by mathematicians for many

Learning Algorithms

decades. Another key feature of reinforcement learning is that it explicitly considers the whole problem of a goal-directed agent interacting with an uncertain environment. This is in contrast with many approaches that address sub-problems without addressing how they might fit into a larger picture. For example, we have mentioned that much of machine learning research is concerned with supervised learning without explicitly specifying how such ability would finally be useful. Other researchers have developed theories of planning with general goals, but without considering planning's role in real-time decision making, or the question of where the predictive models necessary for planning would come from. Although these approaches have yielded many useful results, their focus on isolated sub-problems is a significant limitation. Reinforcement learning takes the opposite tack, by starting with a complete, interactive, goal-seeking agent. All reinforcement learning agents have explicit goals, can sense aspects of their environments and can choose actions to influence their environments.

Moreover, it is usually assumed from the beginning that the agent has to operate despite significant uncertainty about the environment it faces. When reinforcement learning involves planning, it has to address the interplay between planning and real-time action selection, as well as the question of how environmental models are acquired and improved. When reinforcement learning involves supervised learning, it does so for very specific reasons that determine which capabilities are critical and which are not. For learning research to make progress, important sub-problems must be isolated and studied, but they should be sub-problems that are motivated by clear roles in complete, interactive, goal-seeking agents, even if all the details of the complete agent cannot yet be filled in.

Gradient Boosting

Gradient boosting, like random forest, is also made from "weak" decision trees. The significant difference is that in gradient boosting, the trees are trained one after another. Each subsequent tree is trained primarily with data that had been incorrectly identified by previous trees. This allows gradient boost to focus less on the easy-to-predict cases and more on difficult cases.

An ensemble is just a collection of predictors which is a mean of all predictions to give a final prediction. The reason we use ensembles is that many different predictors trying to predict same target variable will perform a better job than any single predictor alone. Ensembling techniques are further classified into Bagging and Boosting.

- Boosting is an ensemble technique in which the predictors are not made independently, but sequentially.
- Bagging is a simple ensembling technique in which we build many independent predictors/models/learners and combine them using some model averaging techniques.

Gradient boosting is an example of boosting algorithm. It is fast to train and performs very well. However, minor changes in the training data set can create radical changes in the model, so it may not produce the most explainable results.

Neural Networks

Neural networks in biology are interconnected neurons that exchange messages with each other. This idea has now been adapted to machine learning and is called artificial neural networks (ANN). Deep learning, which is a recent concept, is just several layers of artificial neural networks put one after the other.

A neural network is a set of connected input-output units where each connection has a weight associated with it. A neural network consists of formal neurons which are connected in such a way that each neuron output further serves as the input of generally more neurons similarly as the axon terminals of a biological neuron are connected via synaptic bindings with dendrites of other neurons. The number of neurons and the way that they are interconnected determine the architecture (topology) of neural network. Regarding their purpose, the input, working (hidden layer, mediate) and output neurons may be distinguished in the network. The input and output neurons represent the receptors and effectors, respectively, and the connected working neurons create the corresponding channels between them to propagate the respective signals. These channels are called paths in the mathematical model. The signal propagation and information processing along a network path is realized by changing the states of neurons on this path. The states of all neurons in the network form the state of the neural network and the synaptic weights associated with all connections represent the configuration of the neural network.

The neural network develops gradually in time, the interconnections as well as the neuron states are being changed, and the weights are being adapted. In the context of updating, these network attributes in time, it is useful to split the global dynamics of neural network into three dynamics and consider three phases of network operation:

1. Architectural (topology change): specifies the network topology and its possible change. The architecture update usually applies within the framework of an adaptive mode in such a way that the network is supplied with additional neurons and connections when it is needed. However, in most cases the architectural dynamics assumes a fixed neural network topology, which is not changed anymore.
2. Computational (state change): specifies the network initial state and a rule for its updates in time, providing that the network topology and configuration are fixed. At the beginning of computational mode, the states of input neurons are assigned to the network input and the remaining neurons find themselves in the initial state. All potential network inputs and states form the input and state space of neural network, respectively. After initializing the network state, a proper computation is performed.

3. Adaptive (configuration change): specifies the network initial configuration and the way that the weights in the network are being adapted in time. All potential network configurations form the weight space of neural network. At the beginning of adaptive mode, the weights of all network connections are assigned to the initial configuration. After initializing the network configuration, the proper adaptation is performed. Likewise, as for the computational dynamics, a model with a continuous time evolution of neural network weights when the configuration is a continuous function of time usually described by a differential equation may generally be considered. However, in most cases a discrete adaptation time is assumed.

This classification does not correspond to neurophysiological reality since in the nervous system all respective changes proceed simultaneously. The above-introduced dynamics of neural network are usually specified by an initial condition and by a mathematical equation or rule that determines the development of a particular network characteristic (topology, state, configuration) in time. The updates controlled by these rules are performed in the corresponding operational modes of neural network. By a concretization of the introduced dynamics, various models of neural networks are obtained which are suitable to solve specific tasks. This means that in order to specify a particular neural network model it suffices to define its architectural, computational and adaptive dynamics.

Neural networks have the ability to classify patterns on data that have not been trained and also, they have better tolerance than other classifier when handling noisy data.

A weakness of neural networks is the difficulty in interpreting its output which comes in symbolic pattern. Other classifier stands better in this regard. A neural network allows for high order variable interactions because of its increased connectivity and tends to handle correlated data better than other learning techniques.

Neural networks have broad applicability to real-world business problems. In fact, they have already been successfully applied in many industries. Since neural networks are best at identifying patterns or trends in data, they are well suited for prediction or forecasting needs including:

- Sales forecasting
- Industrial process control
- Customer research
- Data validation
- Risk management
- Target marketing

There are a variety of benefits that an analyst realizes from using neural networks in his work.

Pattern recognition is a powerful technique for harnessing the information in the data and generalizing about it. Neural networks learn to recognize the patterns which exist in the data set. The system is developed through learning rather than programming. Programming is much more time consuming for the analyst and requires the analyst to specify the exact behaviour of the model. Neural networks teach themselves the patterns in the data, freeing the analyst for interesting work.

Neural networks are flexible in a changing environment. Rule-based systems or programmed systems are limited to the situation for which they were designed – when conditions change, they are no longer valid. Although neural networks may take some time to learn a sudden drastic change, they are excellent at adapting to constantly changing information.

Neural networks can build informative models where more conventional approaches fail. Because neural networks can handle very complex interactions, they can easily model data which is too difficult to model with traditional approaches such as inferential statistics or programming logic.

Performance of neural networks is at least as good as classical statistical modelling and better for most problems. The neural networks build models that are more reflective of the structure of the data in significantly less time.

Neural networks now operate well with modest computer hardware. Although neural networks are computationally intensive, the routines have been optimized to the point that they can now run in reasonable time on personal computers. They do not require super computers as they did in the early days of neural network research.

There are some limitations to neural computing. The key limitation is the neural network's inability to explain the model it has built in a useful way. Analysts often want to know why the model is behaving as it is. Neural networks get better answers, but they have a hard time explaining how they got there. This is the reason neural connection provides so many tools for exploring output and so many operational choices on the tools which build the model. By experimenting with different parameters, and fully exploring the results both in text and graphics, neural connection users can gain more understanding of the model's behaviour and more confidence in the results.

There are a few other limitations that should be understood. First, it is difficult to extract rules from neural networks. This is sometimes important to the people who have to explain their answer to others and to those who have been involved with artificial intelligence, particularly expert systems which are rule based.

In most analytical methods, you cannot just throw data at a neural network and get a conclusive answer, but you have to spend time understanding the problem or the outcome you are trying to predict. And, you must be sure that the data used to train the system are appropriate (i.e. reflects factors involved) and are measured in a way that reflects the behaviour of the factors. If the data are not representative of the problem, neural computing will not produce good results. This is a classic situation where "garbage in" will certainly produce "garbage out".

Finally, it can take time to train a model from a very complex data set. Neural techniques are computer intensive and will be slow on low-end PCs or machines without math coprocessors. It is important to remember though that the overall time to result can still be faster than other data analysis approaches, even when the system takes longer to train. Processing speed alone is not the only factor in performance, and neural networks do not require the time programming and debugging or testing assumptions that other analytical approaches do.

Deep Learning

Introduction

Deep learning consists of many hierarchical layers to process the information in nonlinear manner, where some lower level concept helps to define the higher-level concepts.

Deep learning is defined as,

> Deep learning is a class of machine learning techniques that exploit many layers of non-linear information processing for supervised or unsupervised feature extraction and transformation, and for pattern analysis and classification.

The shallow artificial neural networks are not capable of handling big amount of complex data, which are obvious in many routine applications such as natural speech, images, information retrieval and other human-like information processing applications. Deep learning is suggested for such applications. With deep learning, it is possible to recognize, classify and categorize patterns in data for a machine with comparatively less efforts. Google is pioneer to experiment deep learning, which is initiated by Andrew Ng.

Deep learning offers human-like multilayered processing in comparison with the shallow architecture. The basic idea of deep learning is to employ hierarchical processing using many layers of architecture. The layers of the architecture are arranged hierarchically. Each layer's input is provided to its adjacent layer after some pre-training. Most of the time, such pretraining of a selected layer is done in unsupervised manner. Deep learning follows distributed approach to manage big data. The approach assumes that the data are generated considering numerous factors, different time and various levels. Deep learning facilitates arrangement and processing of the data into different layers according to its time (occurrence), its level or nature. Deep learning is often associated with artificial neural network.

There are three categories of deep learning architectures:

(i) Generative
(ii) Discriminative
(iii) Hybrid deep learning architectures

Architectures belong to the generative category focus on pretraining of a layer in unsupervised manner. This approach eliminates the difficulty of training the lower level architectures, which relay on the previous layers. Each layer can be pretrained and later included into the model for further general tuning and learning. Doing this resolves the problem of training neural network architecture with multiple layers and enables deep learning. Neural network architecture may have discriminative processing ability by stacking output of each layer with the original data or by various information combinations and thus forming deep learning architecture. The descriptive model often considers the neural network outputs as conditional distribution over all possible label sequences for the given input sequence, which will be optimized further through an objective function. The hybrid architecture combines the properties of the generative and discriminative architecture. The typical deep learning can be done as follows.

- *Construct* a network consisting of an input layer and a hidden layer with necessary nodes
- *Train* the network
- *Add* another hidden layer on the top of the previously learned network to generate a new network
- *Retrain* the network
- *Repeat* adding more layers and after every addition, retrain the network (Fig. 1)

Analysing Big Data

The big data analytics is required to manage massive amounts of data efficiently. The major aspects that can be considered while dealing with big data are large-scale optimization, high-dimensional data handling and dynamical data handling. Optimization deals with finding the most effective solution to the problems using well-defined procedures and models. Everybody deals with the problem of optimization either in direct (systematic) way or indirect (informal) way. The problems which need optimization include travelling salesperson problem, selecting a course from available courses under given stream (say science stream) and level (undergraduate), e-commerce activities (choice of best mobile through various online shopping sites), etc.

Optimization helps in finding the cost-effective alternatives to perform the task. Usually, it is considered as maximization or minimization of a function of resources. Some examples are maximization of profit, minimization of cost and errors. For domains with finite dimension, various models for such problem are available; how-

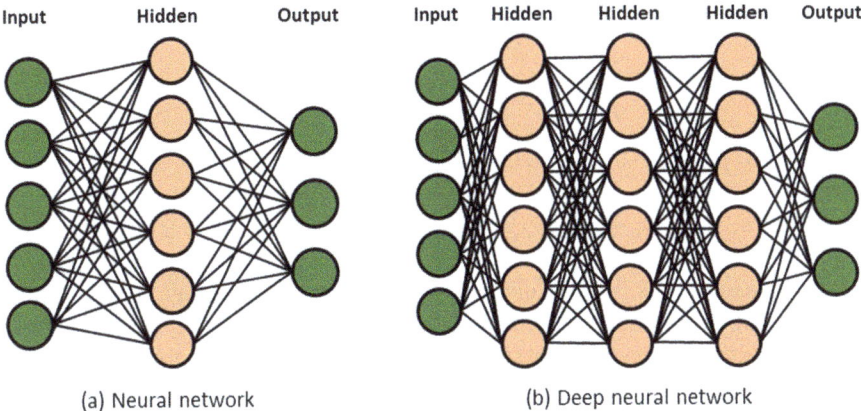

Fig. 1 ANN for deep learning

ever, when it comes to the big data, task of optimization becomes challenging. In case of the big data, not only the size of transactions is voluminous, but the number of variables and number of constraints are also high. On the contrary, sometimes data and constraints are moderate but their structure is complex, in a way that it cannot be handled with the current methods. For example, feature learning from the large repository of medical images in optimum manner will be difficult with support of the traditional method. Further it would require manual tuning of some parameters. Besides traditional approaches, machine learning and parallel optimization methods are also becoming popular. When dimensions in the problem increases, the complexity also does. Limited dimension of the problem makes the problem easy to solve; however, the solution is not powerful and does not provide any high-level knowledge. Increased number of dimensions results in tremendous growth of data which are difficult to handle, visualize and solve. It is said that due to exponential growth of number of possible values with each dimension, complete enumeration of all subspaces becomes intractable with increased dimensionality, which is known as the curse of dimensionality. Deep learning will be helpful in managing such high-dimensional data and help in clustering, processing and visualizing such data. Bioinformatics, sensor web, vision and speech recognition are fields where one can find such high-dimensional data. Besides the volume and structure, time is another major factor that increases the complexity in the data and hence makes the job of managing data more difficult. Dynamic data are varying in terms of size, volume and underlying structure. Large-scale and dynamic data are generated and manipulated in many areas such as fluid dynamics, material science, modular dynamics and bio-inspired systems. An example domain is human speech generation. Human speech generation follows hierarchical structure. Deep learning would be useful in modelling structured speech.

Different Deep Learning Models

Autoencoders

An autoencoder is an artificial neural network capable of learning various coding patterns. The simple form of the autoencoder is just like the multilayer perceptron containing an input layer, one or more hidden layers and an output layer. The major difference between the typical multilayer perceptron and feedforward neural network and autoencoder is in the number of nodes at the output layer. In case of the autoencoder, the output layer contains same number of nodes as in the input layer. Instead of predicting target values as per the output vector, the autoencoder has to predict its own inputs. The broad outline of the learning mechanism is as follows.

```
For each input x,
 - Do a feedforward pass to compute activation functions provided
   at all the hidden layers and output layers
 - Find the deviation between the calculated values with the inputs
   using appropriate error function
 - Backpropagate the error in order to update weights
Repeat the task till satisfactory output.
```

If the number of nodes in the hidden layers is fewer than the input/output nodes, then the activations of the last hidden layer are considered as a compressed representation of the inputs. When the hidden layer nodes are more than the input layer, an autoencoder can potentially learn the identity function and become useless in majority of the cases.

Deep Belief Net

Deep belief network is a solution to the problem of handling non-convex objective functions and local minima while using the typical multilayer perceptron. This is an alternative type of deep learning consisting of multiple layers of latent variables with connection between the layers. The deep belief network can be viewed as restricted Boltzmann machines (RBM) where each subnetwork's hidden layer acts as the visible input layer for the adjacent layer of the network. It makes the lowest visible layer a training set for the adjacent layer of the network. This way, each layer of the network is trained independently and greedily. The hidden variables are used as the observed variables to train each layer of the deep structure. The training algorithm for such deep belief network is provided as follows:

- Consider a vector of inputs
- Train a restricted Boltzmann machine using the input vector and obtain the weight matrix

- Train the lower two layers of the network using this weight matrix
- Generate new input vector by using the network (RBM) through sampling or mean activation of the hidden units
- Repeat the procedure till the top two layers of the network are reached

The fine-tuning of the deep belief network is very similar to the multilayer perceptron. Such deep belief networks are useful in acoustic modelling.

Convolutional Neural Networks

Convolutional neural network (CNN) is another variant of the feedforward multilayer perceptron. It is a type of feedforward neural network, where the individual neurons are arranged in such a way that they respond to overlapping regions in the visual field.

Deep CNNs work by consecutively modelling small pieces of information and combining them deeper in network. One way to understand them is that the first layer will try to detect edges and form templates for edge detection. Then subsequent layers will try to combine them into simpler shapes and eventually into templates of different object positions, illumination, scales, etc. The final layers will match an input image with all the templates and the final prediction is like a weighted sum of all of them. So, deep CNNs can model complex variations and behaviour giving highly accurate predictions.

Such network follows the visual mechanism of the living organisms. The cells in the visual cortex are sensitive to small subregions of the visual field, called a receptive field. The subregions are arranged to cover the entire visual field, and the cells act as local filters over the input space. Backpropagation algorithm is used to train the parameters of each convolution kernel. Further, each kernel is replicated over the entire image with the same parameters. There are convolutional operators which extract unique features of the input. Besides the convolutional layer, the network contains rectified linear unit layer, pooling layers to compute the max or average value of a feature over a region of the image, and a loss layer consisting of application specific loss functions. Image recognition and video analysis and natural language processing are major applications of such neural network.

The area of computer vision has witnessed frequent progresses in the past few years. One of the most stated advancements is CNNs. Now, deep CNNs form the core of most sophisticated fancy computer vision application, such as self-driving cars, auto-tagging of friends in our Facebook pictures, gesture recognition, facial security features, and automatic number plate recognition.

Recurrent Neural Networks

The convolutional model works on fixed number of inputs, generates a fix sized vector as output with predefined number of steps. The recurrent networks allow us to operate over sequences of vectors in input and in output. In case of recurrent neural network, the connection between units forms a directed cycle. Unlike the traditional neural network, the recurrent neural network input and output are not independent but related. Further, the recurrent neural network shares the common parameters at every layer. One can train the recurrent network in a way which is like the traditional neural network using backpropagation method. Here, calculation of gradient depends not on the current step but on previous steps also. A variant called bidirectional recurrent neural network is also used for many applications. The bidirectional neural network not only considers the previous but also the expected future output. In bidirectional and simple recurrent neural networks, deep learning can be achieved by introducing multiple hidden layers. Such deep networks provide higher learning capacity with lots of learning data. Speech, image processing and natural language processing are some of the candidate areas where recurrent neural networks can be used.

Reinforcement Learning to Neural Networks

Reinforcement learning is a kind of hybridization of dynamic programming and supervised learning. Typical components of the approach are environment, agent, actions, policy and cost functions. The agent acts as a controller of the system; policy determines the actions to be taken; and the reward function specifies the overall objective of the reinforcement learning problem.

An agent that receives the maximum possible reward can be viewed as performing the best action for a given state. An agent here refers to an abstract entity which can be any kind of object or subject that performs actions: autonomous cars, robots, humans, customer support chat bots, etc. The state of an agent refers to the agent's position and state of being in its abstract environment; for example, a certain position in a virtual reality world, a building, a chess board, or the position and speed on a racetrack. Deep reinforcement learning holds the promise of a very generalized learning procedure which can learn useful behavior with very little feedback. It is an exciting but also challenging area which will certainly be an important part of the future AI landscape.

Applications of Deep Learning in Business

Analytics has been changing the bottom line for businesses for quite some time. Now that more companies are mastering their use of analytics, they are delving deeper into their data to increase efficiency, gain a greater competitive advantage and boost their bottom lines even more. That is why companies are looking to implement machine learning and artificial intelligence; they want a more comprehensive analytics strategy to achieve these business goals. Learning how to incorporate modern machine learning techniques into their data infrastructure is the first step. For this many are looking to companies that already have begun the implementation process successfully.

Precisely, businesses in the customer engagement space utilize AI and machine learning to analyse conversations, both those that end in a sale and those that do not, and to automatically identify the language that naturally leads to a sale or that predicts when a sale will occur.

An important problem is whether to utilize the entire big data input corpus available when analysing data with deep learning algorithms. The general focus is to apply deep learning algorithms to train the high-level data representation patterns based on a portion of the available input corpus, and then utilize the remaining input corpus with the learnt patterns for extracting the data abstractions and representations. In the context of this problem, a question to explore is what volume of input data is generally necessary to train useful (good) data representations by deep learning algorithms which can then be generalized for new data in the specific big data application domain.

One of the most widely discussed deep learning business applications right now is with self-driving cars – a concept every big player is getting on, from Volkswagen to Google. These systems use sensors and a neural network to process a vast amount of data. The car learns how to recognize obstacles and react appropriately, increasing its knowledge through use beyond its factory programming. The self-driving car systems use sensors and a neural network to process a vast amount of data.

Eventually, given enough data, the machines learn how to drive better than humans.

Another common use is image detection and object classification, as seen today with Facebook. The company has more than enough data on images to work with, making deep learning for image detection very accessible. Currently, Facebook can classify different objects in an image with a very high accuracy.

Business Use Case Example: Deep Learning for e-Commerce

Massive amounts of data are available via mobile e-commerce. This data has allowed deep learning algorithms to trace the buyer journey and by doing that machines now have a clear picture of what kind of product information buyers search for when they are making purchase decisions for different things. Because the machines can hold and reference massive amounts of information at once while applying learned knowledge, they are able to predict what kind of purchases consumers are likely to make before they have made a decision.

What that means is that by following a user's activity, your e-commerce site can offer the buyer purchase options that will appeal to them based on the specifications of other items they have viewed, how much time they spent viewing each item and what they did before and after viewing each item. It will even consider time of day and your viewer's location, whether they are male or female and any other relevant contexts available to the machine.

Let us say Rita is visiting an online store and looking at Blue ladies running shoes. The shoes she is looking at are pretty but not exactly what she wants. She wants a shoe that has more arch support. Fortunately for Rita the site uses deep learning algorithms. Rita can click on the image of the shoe and she will be offered visually comparable products to browse through. The products recommended for her were chosen by analysing the image Rita clicked on, along with her other activity since she entered the site. The algorithm has suggested other pairs of shoes with similar colour and shape characteristics.

The system has worked with an input–output system whereby Rita's actions and preferences have acted as the input, and the shoes that are recommended to her act as the output. The collection of pixels in the image that Rita clicked on serves as inputs, forcing the system to try and find similar sets of data.

It is clear how this is a powerful way of not only marketing your products but of offering client service without even being present. The customer finds what they want easily, they have multiple options presented to them and all the information they may need is readily available. Basically, your e-commerce site becomes like a virtual store assistant.

Deep learning means more opportunities to increase business conversion rates and improve brand image through a positive customer experience. Not only are your customers being served targeted personalized content for the purchase they are making, they are also being offered related products that they are highly likely to be interested in, based on their own individual behaviour.

While deep learning has been effectively applied to challenging pattern inference tasks, the actual purpose of the field is far beyond task-specific applications. This scope may make the comparison of various methodologies increasingly complex and will likely demand a joint effort by the research community to address. Moreover, in spite of the boundless prospect offered by deep learning technologies, some domain-specific tasks may not be directly enhanced by such schemes. Deep learning platforms can also benefit from engineered features while learning more complex representations which engineered systems usually lack. Despite the numerous open research questions and the fact that the field is still in its infancy, advancements made with respect to developing deep learning systems will shape the future of machine learning and artificial intelligence systems at large.

Recommendation Engines

Introduction

Recommendation systems have been emerging as a significant area of research since the mid-1990s. Interest in this research area remains high because, on the one hand, such applications assist users in finding relevant items, and on the other hand, these systems are useful for retrieving items that cannot be accessed because users do not know of their existence. Examples of such applications include recommendations of movies, news and books and other products on Amazon.com.

Recommendation systems were originally developed to suggest items or services that were tailored to the preferences of individual users. However, situations exist in which a group of users collectively participates in a single activity, such as watching a movie or sightseeing in a city. For such cases, we require techniques that address the problem of identifying recommendations for a group of users and satisfying almost all individuals in the group to the greatest extent possible.

One motivation for group recommendation systems; areas related to social choice (also called group decision making) in economics, politics and sociology, in which we wish to decide what is best for a group given the differing opinions of its constituent individuals, also illustrate the importance of group recommendations.

The problem of group recommendation has also been studied in the areas of metasearch, database middleware, collaborative filtering and multi-agent systems. For example, in metasearch, the ranking lists produced by multiple search engines must be combined into one list; this problem is known as the problem of rank aggregation. Database middleware involves the ordering of objects when each object is assigned numerical values related to multiple fields. In multi-agent systems, agents must utilize decisions that are rational not only from an individual's point of view but also from a social point of view. Therefore, we can say that group recommendation attempts to identify items that will be welcomed by a group as a whole rather than simply by individual group members. The groups of interest can vary from established groups to random groups that require only occasional recommendations.

Most research on group recommendation focuses on investigating the core algorithms that are used for recommendation generation. Thus far, two main strategies have been used to generate group recommendations. These techniques involve aggregating individual predictions into group predictions (aggregated predictions) or aggregating individual models into group models (aggregated models).

These strategies differ in the timing of the data aggregation step. In the aggregated prediction strategy, individual predictions are generated based on individual preference models and are then aggregated into a group prediction. An alternative strategy is to construct a group preference model prior to performing item recommendation. In other words, in the aggregated model strategy, individual user models are merged into a group-based model, and recommendations are then generated using the aggregated group model. However, numerous studies have demonstrated that group recommendation is a considerably more complex task than is individual recommendation, and various challenges arise when groups are considered that prevent the traditional recommendation techniques from performing efficiently for the recommendation of items to groups.

Recommendation systems are tools and techniques that provide suggestions for items to be used by users. Recommendation systems are generally directed towards helping users find items in which they are likely to be interested from among an overwhelming number of items; such systems attempt to predict the most suitable products or services based on the users' preferences and constraints.

The general classification of data that is used by recommendation systems utilizes three categories: items, users and transactions, that is, relations between users and items.

1. Items are the objects that are recommended. Items may be characterized in terms of their complexity and their value or utility.
2. Users of a recommendation system may have very diverse goals and characteristics. To personalize its recommendations, a recommendation system attempts to exploit information about its users. This information can be structured in many ways; the selection of which information to model depends on the recommendation technique being used.
3. A transaction is a recorded interaction between a user and the recommendation system. Transactions are data that are useful to the recommendation generation algorithm. Ratings are the most popular form of transaction data that a recommendation system collects. Other types of transaction data may include reading history or how often a user takes advantage of the recommendations with which she has provided. Ratings may take a variety of forms, such as numerical ratings, ordinal ratings and binary ratings.

Recommendation systems can be used for a variety of purposes, as stated by when identifying typical tasks with which a recommendation system can assist, such as the topics listed below.

- Finding desirable items: This task involves finding a ranked list of items for a user and predicting how much the user will like the items (e.g. star ratings).
- Finding all desirable items: This task involves finding all, not simply some, of the items in which a user will be interested. It is sometimes necessary to find all possible items for a user, not simply some of them. Examples include medical, financial and legal situations, in which false positives could potentially have huge consequences if present.
- Providing annotation in context: This task involves finding useful items in the current context of the user. For example, a system could provide recommendations such as "Customers who bought this item in this specific context (Christmas) also bought this" or "Similar movies" when the user is searching for a movie.
- Finding a recommended sequence: This task involves finding a sequence of items for a user that is "pleasant as a whole" instead of matching the user's preferences only in terms of individual components. Examples of such recommendation systems include song playlist generation and the radio function in Spotify.
- Simple browsing: This task involves assisting users who wish to browse a set of items by providing suggestions that are relevant to them. Such recommendations are offered by various services, including Amazon.com and eBay.
- Finding a credible recommender: Some users tend not to trust recommendation systems. They can experiment with the system and observe how the system behaves in different settings by, for example, changing their profile. Recommendation systems can help to assert their credibility by also including the reason that a given item in the results was recommended, for example, "this song was recommended because you listened to xy".
- Improving one's profile by rating items: A user can help to improve the outcome of the recommendation algorithm by allowing the algorithm to gain a better understanding of the types of items that the user likes.
- Expressing oneself: Users can also rate items because they enjoy doing so, because they like to express themselves and feel good about it. Here, the main goal is not to improve the results of the recommendation system but to express one's feelings about an item.
- Helping others: The main goal of rating an item might also be to help others. If a user, for example, has had a bad experience with a tour company, posting a response and a rating on a website such as tripadvisor.com to warn others might be a motivation for the user to use the recommendation system.
- Influencing others: Recommendation systems can be used to promote a business. Sites such as hotels.com and tripadvisor.com can be used to assign ratings to hotels, among other facilities and services. Unethical approaches, such as encouraging individuals (e.g. employees) to assign large volumes of high ratings to one business while assigning lower ratings to its competitors, can be used to promote a business.

Recommendation System Techniques

Recommendation techniques may utilize several different classifications. These classifications are based on the data that are used as input for recommendation. In the following sections, we will present such a classification that is proposed in the literature and will provide a survey on diverse types of recommender systems. Recommender systems are usually classified into the following categories, based on how recommendation is made:

Content-Based Recommendations

Content-based approach has its foundation in information retrieval and is based on the idea that users will prefer items that are like items of which they have previously expressed enjoyment. Content-based recommendation systems analyse item descriptions to identify items that are particularly interesting to the user, and they focus on the features of the items.

The similarity of items is determined by measuring the similarity of their features. Indeed, recommendation systems attempt to recommend items that are similar to items that a given user has liked in the past. Such a system analyses a set of features of the items that have been previously rated by a user and constructs a model or profile of the user's interests based on the features of the items rated by that user. For instance, such a model could be used to filter search results by deciding whether a user is interested in a specific web page.

An example of such a recommendation would be the recommendation of a particular hotel based on its number of stars or price level or whether it offers outdoor services. A content-based filtering algorithm for hotel recommendations can be conceptually described as follows:

The system collects a set of features in combination with the probability that each user will like each feature. To determine a hotel that the user will most likely prefer, the system performs a comparison between this feature set and the various hotels in the system. The comparison can include heuristics or simply a similarity calculation such as a cosine-based calculation. The system then returns the hotels that represent the best fit to the user's preferences. Content-based filtering can be very useful when a substantial amount of descriptive data is available for the items. These data can be codified and internally represented as an ontology of features, thereby providing a detailed description of the domain that is applicable to the similarity calculation against the user's preferences. Nevertheless, to be useful, a content-based scheme must have such an ontology available in addition to the ability to classify items according to the ontology. Therefore, content-based filtering can be problematic when the information that is available for each item is sparse or difficult to interpret using computer algorithms. Furthermore, content-based recommendations can only be based on the available explicit information regarding a certain item.

Several components, such as item representations, user profiles and the ability to learn a user model, are present in the high-level architecture of content-based filtering; these components will be explained in detail below.

Item Representations

Items that can be recommended to users are represented by a set of features. For instance, each movie is associated with certain features, such as genres, actors, subjects and dates. When each item is described by a set of features and the values of these features are known, the items can be represented by structured data. When the data have no structure, as is the case for text, a preprocessing step is required to extract relevant structured information. The primary task of such a component is to represent the contents of the items, for example, documents, web pages, news items and product descriptions, in a form that is suitable for use in the subsequent processing steps. Data items are analysed using feature extraction techniques to shift the item representations from the original information space to the target space. For example, web pages can be represented as keyword vectors.

User Profiles

This component creates a model based on user interest inferred from previous likes and dislikes of items. Typically, the generalization strategy is implemented using machine learning techniques, which are able to infer a model of user interests from items that have been liked or disliked in the past. For instance, for news recommendations based on a user's reading history, various properties of news articles, such as news content, access patterns and named entities, can be incorporated to construct a user profile. This profile is then used as a representation of the item for use in identifying items that are suitable for a target user. This representation typically consists of a vector of weighted features: the greater the weight, the more the user likes the feature. The size of the vector corresponds to the number of features. Several approaches exist that can be used to build user profiles from item profiles. It is possible to compute each user profile as an average vector based on the profiles of items evaluated by the user.

Learning of User Models

This module exploits the user's profile to suggest relevant items by matching the profile representation against those of items to be recommended. The result may be based on a binary or a continuous relevance judgement using various similarity metrics.

Collaborative Recommendations

In this approach, instead of using the features of items to determine their similarity, the focus is placed on the similarity of user ratings for items. For example, in movie recommendations, to predict the rating by user u of movie i, the collaborative filtering technique attempts to identify users that are similar to u, that is, other users who have similar tastes in movies (i.e. they rate the same movies similarly). Then, the technique aggregates the ratings expressed by users with similar rating patterns and computes a predicted rating for a given user.

Collaborative filtering is by far the most widespread recommendation technique because of its power and simplicity. The greatest strength of collaborative techniques is that they are completely independent of any machine-readable representation of the objects being recommended and can be effectively applied to complex objects, such as music and movies, which a user may like or dislike for numerous reasons. For example, a user might like a certain genre of movies, a specific director, a specific actor or actress, etc. Collaborative filtering is often referred to as social filtering because the technique recognizes commonalities among users on the basis of their ratings and generates new recommendations based on inter-user comparisons. This process mimics the social process of recommending items to friends because the system provides recommendations to users based on the items that people who are similar to the user in terms of ratings have liked in the past.

Algorithms used in collaborative filtering systems can be grouped into two general classes: memory-based (or heuristic-based) and model-based algorithms.

Memory-based algorithms provide rating predictions for users based on their past ratings. Memory-based approaches apply heuristics that use all or a sample of user–item data to generate a prediction. Two general approaches to memory-based collaborative filtering (CF) are used: user-based collaborative filtering and item-based collaborative filtering. User-based collaborative filtering produces predictions for a given user by first identifying users who are similar (nearest neighbours) to the given user and then computing the most frequently rated items that the given user has not seen. For example, a collaborative filtering recommendation system for books could suggest a book that has not been read by a given user but that has been read by users with similar taste. Item-based collaborative filtering produces predictions for a given user by first computing the most similar items to each item according to their similarities.

Model-based algorithms model users based on their past ratings, and recommender systems then use these models to predict the ratings of unrated items. In this method, after the algorithm learns the model, it no longer needs access to every rating and can use the model parameters to compute its predictions. Model-based approaches (such as machine learning and data mining algorithms) are used to design and develop models that allow the system to learn complex patterns based on training data and then provide predictions based on the models thus learned. The advantage of this approach is that after the model is learned, the system no longer requires access to every rating, and the model parameters can be used to compute predictions; however, the learning phase can be time consuming. By contrast, memory-based approaches are slower during the prediction phase because they must heuristically explore the complete set of ratings, whereas model-based approaches are quite fast because they use only the model parameters to compute the predicted rating.

Hybrid Approaches

Another popular method of formulating recommendations is the use of a hybrid approach. One can either separately implement collaborative and content-based systems and combine the results, thus incorporating characteristics from one method into the other method or create a unifying model that possesses characteristics of both approaches. The use of such a technique helps to mitigate certain limitations of content-based and collaborative systems.

- Implementing collaborative and content-based methods separately and combining their predictions
- Incorporating some content-based characteristics into a collaborative approach
- Incorporating some collaborative characteristics into a content-based approach
- Constructing a general unifying model that incorporates both content-based and collaborative characteristics

Applications of Recommendation Engines in Business

If you have used the streaming service of Netflix, bought something from Amazon or connected with "people you may know" on LinkedIn or Facebook, then you have used a recommendation engine.

Recommendation engines match features about you with things that you might be interested in. For instance, a movie has a release year, a genre, actors and box office results. You have features. You have preferences, an age, and you may have completed a survey expressing some of your attitudes towards certain movies. You may have rated some of the movies you watched. By figuring out which sets of movies to show you, and your response to those recommendations, the machine learns over time to make better suggestions. If you watched a few science fiction movies, and you rated them highly, then the engine will learn to show you more science fiction movies, and, for variety, movies that other people like you, who like science fiction movies, might also enjoy. Recommendation systems have been deployed across a wide range of industries and contexts, especially as part of online shopping sites, explained Thompson. You will typically see them used in:

- Supermarkets: Registers that generate custom coupons for next purchases look at prior purchases and tailor coupons to include items you would likely be interested in.
- Book and music stores: Companies can send customers emails following a purchase and recommend new books or albums – or in the case of Amazon, Pandora and similar sites, provide product recommendations in real time based on what a customer is currently looking at or listening to.
- Investment firms: Recommendation systems can analyse which stocks you would likely be interested in based on what similar customers have chosen.
- TV and movie services: Companies like Netflix analyse each customer's prior content choices and make recommendations based on them, as well as proactively recommend items in real time based on their browsing history.
- Social network sites: Sites like LinkedIn and Facebook use recommendation systems to suggest additional connections or friends based on a person's existing network.

Many of the algorithms that are used in recommendation engines and machine learning are not all that new. Regression, decision trees, k-nearest neighbour, support vector machines (SVMs), neural networks and naive Bayes are established methods with well-known constraints and appropriate uses. Many of these methods have been used to support data-driven business decision making for a long time. A typical recommendation engine processes data through the following four phases namely collection, storing, analysing and filtering.

Collection of Data

The first step in creating a recommendation engine is gathering data. Data can be either explicit or implicit data. Explicit data would consist of data inputted by users such as ratings and comments on products. And implicit data would be the order history/return history, Cart events, Pageviews, Click thru and search log. This data set will be created for every user visiting the site.

Behaviour data is easy to collect because you can keep a log of user activities on your site. Collecting this data is also straightforward because it does not need any extra action from the user; they are already using the application. The downside of this approach is that it is harder to analyse the data. For example, filtering the needful logs from the less needful ones can be cumbersome.

Since each user is bound to have different likes or dislikes about a product, their data sets will be distinct. Over time as you "feed" the engine more data, it gets smarter and smarter with its recommendations so that your email subscribers and customers are more likely to engage, click and buy. Just like how the Amazon's recommendation engine works with the "Frequently bought together" and "Recommended for you" tab.

Storing the Data

The more data you can make available to your algorithms, better the recommendations will be. This means that any recommendations project can quickly turn into a big data project.

The type of data that you use to create recommendations can help you decide the type of storage you should use. You could choose to use a NoSQL database, a standard SQL database or even some kind of object storage. Each of these options is viable depending on whether you are capturing user input or behaviour and on factors such as ease of implementation, the amount of data that the storage can manage, integration with the rest of the environment and portability.

When saving user ratings or comments, a scalable and managed database minimizes the number of tasks required and helps to focus on the recommendation.

Analysing the Data

In order to find items that have similar user engagement data, we filter the data by using different analysis methods. If you want to provide immediate recommendations to the user as they are viewing the product then you will need a nimbler type of analysis. Some of the ways in which we can analyse the data are: Real-time systems can process data as it is created. This type of system usually involves tools that can process and analyse streams of events. A real-time system would be required to give in-the-moment recommendations. Batch analysis demands you to process the data periodically. This approach implies that enough data needs to be created in order to make the analysis relevant, such as daily sales volume. A batch system might work fine to send an email at a later date. Near-real-time analysis lets you gather data quickly, so you can refresh the analytics every few minutes or seconds. A near-real-time system works best for providing recommendations during the same browsing session.

Product Recommendation Algorithm

```
Filtering the data: To get the relevant data necessary to provide
recommendations to the user. We have to choose an algorithm that
would better suit the recommendation engine.
Content-based: A popular, recommended product has similar charac-
teristics to what a user views or likes.
Cluster: Recommended products go well together, no matter what
other users have done.
Collaborative: Other users, who like the same products as another
user views or likes, will also like a recommended product.
Collaborative filtering enables you to make product attributes
theoretical and make predictions based on user tastes.
The output of this filtering is based on the assumption that two
users who liked the same products in the past will probably like
the same ones now or in the future.
```

You can represent data about ratings or interactions as a set of matrices, with products and users as dimensions. Assume that the following two matrices are similar, but then we deduct the second from the first by replacing existing ratings with the number one and missing ratings by the number zero. The resulting matrix is a truth table where a number one represents an interaction by users with a product.

Ultimately, the result obtained after filtering and using the algorithm, recommendations are given to the user based on the timeliness of the type of recommendation, whether real-time recommendation or sending an email later after some time.

Since a product recommendation engine mainly runs on data. Business may not have the storage capacity to store this enormous amount of data from visitors on your site. One can use online frameworks like Hadoop and Spark which allows you to store data in multiple devices to reduce dependability on one machine. Hadoop uses HDFS to split files into large blocks and distributes them across nodes in a cluster. This allows the data set to be processed faster and more efficiently than it would be in a more conventional supercomputer architecture that relies on a parallel file system where computation and data are distributed via high-speed networking.

Finally, we process big data sets using the MapReduce programming model. With this, we can run the algorithm in the distributed file system at the same time and choose the most similar cluster. Thus, any business can develop its own recommendation engine architecture using open source tools, and we can help them in implementing the engine using our technical expertise.

Business Use Case

Recommendation engines play a critical role in customer engagement and retention for online media and entertainment industry. With the exponential volume of media data, recommendation engines with big data demonstrate a modern, user-centric media delivery approach through efficient data processing, machine learning and predictive analytics. A media recommendation engine can be built for movies or music videos, books or any products.

Such movie video (big) data use case focuses on a recommendation engine architecture for consumers who use set-top box (STB), which:

- Uses the open source Hadoop architecture as the big data underpinning
- Gathers raw user data from on-demand videos, set top box activity logs, scheduled recordings and several media catalogs
- Processes and analyses user log data within the Hadoop big data framework
- Feeds the results into a search engine which then delivers unique recommendations via a user-facing browser interface

At a granular level, individual user behaviours, such as the videos watched, the catalogues clicked on, the programs scheduled for recording, average video view time, are thoroughly analysed following a big data log analytics methodology. At a high level, this enormous data can paint a picture of "what's hot" for a particular user or among groups of users with similar tastes.

For data analysts, this recommendation engine architecture goes beyond running SQL queries against a data warehouse to predict trends and preferences. Big data allows them to be more efficient by processing enormous amounts of user data in a fraction of time compared to traditional SQL. The personalized results were loaded onto a search engine and displayed on an in-built web application.

For marketers, this is an excellent tool for mining user personas and delivering what users want.

For end users, personalized recommendations save them the manual work of browsing through a huge database of videos. Machine learning and predictive analytics enable the recommendation engine to become more accurate at predicting users' preferences, that is, boosting user satisfaction and retention.

Big data, with its scalability and power to process massive amounts of both structured (e.g. video titles users search for, music genre they prefer) and unstructured data (e.g. user viewing/listening patterns), can enable companies to analyse billions of clicks and viewing data from you and other users like you for the best recommendations.

While recommendation engines have been widely adopted and studied for over a decade, a few key challenges remain.

Scalability: The amount of data used as input to recommendation engines is growing fast as more users and items are added. For example, for a popular website the size of stored user behavior data can easily reach terabytes per day. Despite the large amount of data, most recommendation engines aspire to respond interactively in less than a second in order to keep users engaged. A main challenge here is to design efficient learning algorithms that can handle such large scale datasets.

Privacy: With an understanding of the value of user data, most websites are collecting as much user data as possible. This approach raises privacy concerns because the data may contain sensitive information that the users wish to keep private, e.g. users' addresses and payment history. Although users are presented with privacy policies concerning the usage of data, they normally have no explicit control over the data.

Sparsity: Sparsity is the problem of lack of information. In online shops that have a huge amount of users and items there are almost always users that have rated just a few items. Using collaborative and other approaches recommendation engines basically create neighborhoods of users using their profiles. If a user has evaluated just few items, then it is pretty difficult to determine his taste and she could be related to the wrong neighborhood.

Structured recommendations: Current recommendation engines predict individual items that users may want. A fascinating extension is to predict preferences for sets of items. For example, if the system figures out that a user is going for winter sports for the first time, it can recommend a pair of boots, helmet, goggles and ski dress that have matching colors and price levels. In this way, a user can obtain everything that she needs for skiing with a single purchase. There are two challenges in this kind of structured recommendations. First, the number of possible sets grows exponentially with the group size. Considering that the number of items is already very large, the efficiency of learning algorithms could be an issue. Second, unlike individual items, it is unclear how to select the right score function for sets.

Trust: The voices of people with a short history may not be that relevant as the voices of those who have rich history in their profiles. The issue of trust arises towards evaluations of a certain customer. The problem could be solved by distribution of priorities to the users.

Natural Language Processing

Introduction

When we communicate with each other we employ, almost effortlessly, very complex and yet little understood processes. It has been very difficult to build computers which can generate and understand even fragments of natural language. This is because, language has developed as an effective communication medium between intelligent beings. It is seen as transmitting a bit of "mental structure" from one brain to another when each brain possesses large, highly similar mental structures that serve as a common context. This similarity in contexts helps in generating and understanding highly condensed messages. Thus, natural language understanding is a highly complex problem of encoding and decoding.

One of the long-standing goals of AI is the creation of programs that are capable of understanding and generating human language. Not only does the ability to use and understand natural language seem to be a fundamental aspect of human intelligence, but also its successful automation would have an incredible impact on the usability and effectiveness of computers themselves. Much effort has been put into writing programs that understand natural language. Although these programs have achieved success within restricted contexts, systems that can use natural language with the flexibility and generality that characterize human speech are beyond current methodologies.

Understanding natural language involves much more than parsing sentences into their individual parts of speech and looking those words up in a dictionary. Real understanding depends on extensive background knowledge about the domain of discourse and the idioms used in that domain as well as an ability to apply general contextual knowledge to resolve the omissions and ambiguities that are a normal part of human speech.

Therefore, in order to build computer systems which can understand natural language, both the contextual knowledge and the process for making effective inferences is required. Natural language processing (NLP) is already transforming business intelligence (BI), in ways that go far beyond simply making the interface easier. Natural language processing is the scientific discipline concerned with making natural language accessible to machines. NLP addresses tasks such as identifying sentence boundaries in documents, extracting relationships from documents and searching and retrieving of documents, among others. NLP is a necessary means to facilitate text analytics by establishing structure in unstructured text to enable further analysis.

The simple understanding is that the sentences of a text are first analysed in terms of their syntax; this provides an order and structure that is more amenable to an analysis in terms of semantics, or literal meaning; and this is followed by a stage of pragmatic analysis whereby the meaning of the utterance or text in context is determined. This last stage is often seen as being concerned with discourse, whereas the previous two are generally concerned with sentential matters. This attempt at a correlation between a stratificational distinction (syntax, semantics and pragmatics) and a distinction in terms of granularity (sentence versus discourse) sometimes causes some confusion in thinking about the issues involved in natural language processing, and it is widely recognized that in real terms it is not so easy to separate the processing of language neatly into boxes corresponding to each of the strata. However, such a separation serves as a useful pedagogic aid and also constitutes the basis for architectural models that make the task of natural language analysis more manageable from a software engineering point of view.

Two problems make the processing of natural languages hard and cause different techniques to be used than those associated with the construction of compilers, etc. for processing artificial languages. These problems are the level of ambiguity that exists in natural languages and the complexity of semantic information contained in even simple sentences.

Basic NLP tasks include tokenization and parsing, lemmatization/stemming, part-of-speech tagging, language detection and identification of semantic relationships.

NLP tasks break down language into shorter, elemental pieces, try to understand relationships between the pieces and explore how the pieces work together to create meaning.

These underlying tasks are often used in higher-level NLP capabilities, such as:

- *Content categorization*: A linguistic-based document summary, including search and indexing, content alerts and duplication detection
- *Topic discovery and modelling:* Accurately capture the meaning and themes in text collections and apply advanced analytics to text, like optimization and forecasting
- *Contextual extraction:* Automatically pull structured information from text-based sources
- *Sentiment analysis:* Identifying the mood or subjective opinions within substantial amounts of text, including average sentiment and opinion mining
- *Speech-to-text and text-to-speech conversion:* Transforming voice commands into written text and vice versa

- *Document summarization:* Automatically generating synopses of large bodies of text
- *Machine translation:* Automatic translation of text or speech from one language to another

In all these cases, the main objective is to take raw language input and use linguistics and algorithms to transform or enrich the text in such a way that it delivers greater value.

A basic view of NLP highlights four distinct stages: morphological processing, syntax analysis (parsing), semantic analysis and pragmatic analysis.

Morphological Processing

The preliminary stage which takes place before syntax analysis is morphological processing. The purpose of this stage of language processing is to break strings of language input into sets of tokens corresponding to discrete words, sub-words and punctuation forms. For example, a word like "discontentedly" can be broken into three sub-word tokens as: `dis- contented -ly`.

Morphology is concerned primarily with recognizing how base words have been modified to form other words with similar meanings but often with different syntactic categories. Modification typically occurs by the addition of prefixes and/or postfixes, but other textual changes can also take place.

Syntax and Semantics

A language processor must carry out several different functions primarily based around syntax analysis and semantic analysis. The purpose of syntax analysis is twofold: to check that a string of words (a sentence) is well formed and to break it up into a structure that shows the syntactic relationships between the different words. A syntactic analyser (or parser) does this using a dictionary of word definitions (the lexicon) and a set of syntax rules (the grammar). A simple lexicon only contains the syntactic category of each word; a simple grammar describes rules which indicate only how syntactic categories can be combined to form phrases of distinct types.

Semantics and Pragmatics

After semantic analysis the next stage of processing deals with pragmatics. Unfortunately, there is no universally agreed distinction between semantics and pragmatics. Semantic analysis associates meaning with isolated utterances/sentences;

pragmatic analysis interprets the results of semantic analysis from the perspective of a specific context. This means that with a sentence like "The large cat chased the rat" semantic analysis can produce an expression which means the large cat but cannot carry out the further step of inference required to identify the large cat as Felix. This would be left up to pragmatic analysis. In some cases, like the example just described, pragmatic analysis simply fits actual objects/events which exist in a given context with object references obtained during semantic analysis. In other cases, pragmatic analysis can disambiguate sentences which cannot be fully disambiguated during the syntax and semantic analysis phases.

Presently, NLP tends to be based on turning natural language into machine language. But as the technology develops – particularly the AI component – the computer will get better at "understanding" the query and start to deliver answers rather than search results.

This is one step further from asking the question in natural language. It is receiving it that way too. But once it learns the semantic relations and inferences of the question, it will be able to automatically perform the filtering and business necessary to provide an intelligible answer, rather than simply showing you data.

Use Cases of NLP

Chatbots have been in the market for several years, but the newer ones have a better understanding of language and are more interactive. Some businesses use chatbots to answer routine questions in help desks. Some use bots to help in routing help desk questions. Here, based on who you are and what you asked for, you will be routed to the right call-centre person to answer your specific questions. Other businesses use it for personalized shopping that involves understanding what you and people like you bought, in addition to what you are searching for. These use cases require smart NLP-based search as well as machine learning.

Most people are familiar with interactive search applications such as Siri or Alexa. However, more frequently, other kinds of applications are using some sort of natural language interface. This includes BI applications where users can ask questions, either by voice or by text, in a natural language fashion and get answers back from the application.

Additionally, machine learning is being used inside of data management and BI applications to help with everything from data integration to data preparation to the actual analytics analysis. Some applications provide users with insights that they may not have thought to look for on their own. Several of the sponsors for this report are providing this kind of functionality.

Using deep learning, a system can be trained to recognize images and sounds. The systems learn from examples that are labelled in order to become accurate in classifying new images or sounds. For instance, a computer can be trained to identify certain sounds that indicate that a motor is failing. This kind of application is being used in cars and aviation. Though we think about auto tagging images in social networks, this kind of technology is also being used to classify photos in business for online auto sales or for identifying other products.

Text Analytics

Text analytics studies the face value of the words, including the grammar and the relationships among the words. Simply put, text analytics gives you the meaning. Sentiment analysis gives insight into the emotion behind the words.

Text analytics refers to the extraction of useful information from text sources. It is a broad term that describes tasks from annotating text sources with meta-information such as people and places mentioned in the text to a wide range of models about the *documents* (e.g. sentiment analysis, text clustering and categorization). To expand, the term *document* is an abstract notion that can represent any coherent piece of text in a larger collection such as a single blog post in a collection of WordPress posts, a newspaper article, a page on Wikipedia and so on.

During text analytics activity, a researcher may develop features that describe several aspects of the document, for example:

- The document is about "health" or "travel".
- The phone call contains of a lot of negative language.
- The website indicates a specific product.
- The tweet describes a relation between a product and a problem with the product.
- The author of the blog post is perhaps physiotherapist.
- The email breaks compliance because it reveals personal information.

A typical text-analytics application in the finance industry focuses on compliance and fraud prevention. The purpose of natural language processing in this use case is to understand the content of communication threads through semantic interpretation and to identify relationships and entities across threads. Text analytics, however, is responsible for determining whether a given message, or set of messages, breaks compliance. Compliance departments benefit from combining structured data, like trades and transactions, alongside the information extracted from emails and instant messages. With both types of data assets, it is then possible to infer the intent behind a transaction.

Financial organizations face another fundamental compliance problem – anti-money laundering. Financial institutions are obligated to screen all transactions across the entirety of their business units to preventing transactions between blacklisted parties. This task involves the analysis of free text contained within the transaction and matching names and entities against watch lists from the Office of Foreign Assets Control (OFAC) and other governmental agencies.

One important task is matching transliterated names to "one" representation on a list. For example, the name Rajendra can be transliterated to Rajinder, Raj, or Raja. The match against multiple lists must be very precise as analysts can only manually review a small percentage of alerts.

In the insurance business, companies have huge collections of unstructured call centre, claim, billing and adjuster notes text data. To get a better understanding of policyholders, these companies can utilize sentiment analysis to gauge if their customers are satisfied or dissatisfied with their products, services and processes. Text analytics can identify problem areas with the products and procedures, and it can provide guidance for improving services or developing new products.

Sentiment Analysis

Sentiment analysis is the use of natural language processing, statistics and text analysis to extract and identify the sentiment of text into positive, negative or neutral categories. We often see sentiment analysis used to arrive at a binary decision: somebody is either for or against something, users like or dislike something or the product is good or bad. There are strategic benefits in knowing consumer sentiment related to your competitors. Sentiment analysis can help predict customer trends, so keeping a pulse on public opinion of other businesses in your industry provides a control group to compare your scores against.

Sentiment analysis is also called opinion mining since it includes identifying consumer attitudes, emotions and opinions of a company's product, brand or service. Sentiment analysis provides insight on any change in public opinion related to your brand that will either support or negate the direction your business is heading. High or low sentiment scores help you identify ways to restructure teams or develop new creative strategies.

Sentiment Analysis Use Cases

The use of sentiment analysis is frequently applied to reviews and social media to help marketing and customer service teams identify the feelings of consumers. In media, such as product reviews, sentiment analysis can be used to uncover whether consumers are satisfied or dissatisfied with a product. Similarly, a firm could use sentiment analysis to measure the impact of a new product, ad campaign or consumer's response to recent company news on social media.

A customer service agent at a company could use sentiment analysis to automatically sort incoming user email into "urgent" or "not urgent" buckets based on the sentiment of the email, proactively identifying frustrated users. The agent could then direct their time towards resolving the users with the most urgent needs first.

Sentiment analysis is often used in business intelligence to understand the subjective reasons why consumers are or are not responding to something (e.g. Why are consumers buying a product? What do they think of the user experience? Did customer service support meet their expectations?). Sentiment analysis can also be used in the areas of political science, sociology and psychology to analyse trends, ideological bias, opinions, gauge reactions, etc.

Challenges of Sentiment Analysis

People express opinions in complex ways, which makes understanding the subject of human opinions a difficult problem to solve. There are several defined elements in a piece of text that factor into sentiment analysis: the object, the attributes, the opinion holder, the opinion orientation and the opinion strength.

```
Object: The product, service, individual, business, event or topic
being analysed
Example: iPhone
Attributes: The specific components and properties of the object
Component examples: Battery, touch screen, headphone jack
Property examples: Size, weight, processing speed
Opinion holder: The person or business who is expressing the
sentiment
Example: The person who purchased the iPhone
Opinion orientation (polarity): The general position of the
opinion
Examples: Positive, negative or neutral
Opinion strength: The level, scale or intensity of the opinion
Examples: Thrilled > jubilant > happy > satisfied
```

To obtain complete, accurate and actionable information from a piece of text, it is important to not only identify each of these five elements individually but to also understand how they work together to provide the full context and sentiment. Because keyword processing only identifies the sentiment reflected in a particular word, it fails at providing all of the elements necessary to understand the complete context of the entire piece.

Applications of NLP in Business

We explore some examples of how NLP business applications can be applied at scale to address business questions.

Customer Service

NLP is used by computers to manipulate human language, whether to extract meaning, generate text or for any other purpose. The interaction computer-language is categorized according to the task that needs to be accomplished: summarizing a long document, translating between two human languages or detecting spam email are all examples of tasks that today can be decently accomplished by a machine.

Most of NLP today is based on machine learning, that is, statistical methods that are able to simulate what a human would do in similar circumstances. NLP is heavily used in customer service.

Relevant NLP tasks in customer service include:

- Speech recognition, which converts spoken language into text
- Question answering, which involves exactly that – Answering questions posed by humans in a natural language

Reputation Monitoring

As the cost of computation kept dropping and algorithms kept improving, businesses started adopting tools that allowed them to look beyond their databases. This kind of data is commonly referred to as external data, public data or open-source intelligence (OSINT). While some of this data is structured and ready to be analysed (e.g. census data, stock prices), most of its value remains tapped in unstructured, human-generated text such as news, blog posts, forums, patents, job postings, reports, social media, and company websites. These sources contain a plethora of precious information about how competitors, customers and the market as a whole are evolving.

Nowadays as consumers have started voicing their complaints on Twitter and Facebook, reputation monitoring and management has become a top priority for businesses. Companies can now scan the entire web for mentions of their brand and products and recognize cases when they should act.

Relevant NLP tasks for this application include:

- Sentiment analysis, which determines the attitude, emotional state, judgement or intent of the writer. This is done by either assigning a polarity to the text (positive, neutral or negative) or trying to recognize the underlying mood (happy, sad, calm, angry, etc.).
- Coreference resolution, which connects pronouns to the right objects. This is a challenging task, but it is indispensable to interpret the text correctly. For example, if a customer writes: "A dude from the seller called to ask if I liked my new apartment. Fine, no man, it sucks?", it is important to recognize that "it" refers to the apartment and not the person. In short, the customer is complaining about the product, not the service.

Ad placement Media buying is typically the major line in a company's advertising budget, so any targeting that can be done to ensure that ads are presented to the right eyeballs is of immense importance. Our emails, social media, e-commerce and browsing behaviours contain a lot of information about what we are interested in. Relevant NLP tasks for this application include:

- Keyword matching, which checks whether words of interest are included in some text. While this first approximation is often good enough, its lack of sophistication can produce pretty inappropriate results.
- Sense disambiguation or identification of which sense of a word is used in a sentence. This is one of the main open problems in NLP.

Market Intelligence

To know the status of an industry is essential to developing an effective strategy, but the channels of content distribution today (RSS feeds, social media, emails) produce so much information that it is becoming hard to keep up. Relevant NLP tasks for this application include:

- Event extraction: which recognizes what is happening to an entity. A structured database of events about companies, governments and people is an extremely powerful tool for analysing the business ecosystem.
- *Sentence classification:* is often used as a first pass to extract relevant content from large repositories.
- *Regulatory compliance:* A crucial example of compliance is the studies done after a drug has been marketed to gather information on its side effects. Relevant NLP tasks for this application include:
- *Named entity recognition*: extracts the names of drugs, diseases, patients and pharma companies using rule-based or statistical methods.
- *Relation detection:* used to identify the context in which the adverse drug event is mentioned. This is often done with frames or patterns of words that correspond to a concept.

Both these tasks benefit from using ontologies, that is, structured domain knowledge that provides the object dictionary and the relations between objects.

Sentiment Technology in Business

To address variation, sentiment technology is most useful when it can be adapted to examine contemporary issues, allowing you to answer a question framed in several diverse ways or ask completely different questions of the same data.

When you can examine a question from different perspectives, you are likely serving a multitude of needs, and often you will want to share analytic results in a variety of ways – say by integrating with your current alert processes, workflows and monitoring reports. Analytic applications have the flexibility to examine all the available information in any number of ways, use different techniques to solve a problem and alternate methods to deliver the derived insights.

For analytic problems like sentiment, you need technology that does not restrict you to examining the question in only one or two ways, with a single definition or with only some of the data. With an integrated approach to analytics, you have the power to get the answers from the data – answers to questions you already have, as well as those you have not even thought to ask yet. If you use instead a highly specialized method – for example, subscribe to a social media report that monitors a trend for you – you are not gaining any kind of competitive differentiation. When the technology is integrated so you can use different methods and approaches, your analytical environment supports innovation.

Having a variety of analysis capabilities at your fingertips is best for solving sentiment questions and, for that matter, any other analytic question. For example, by including predefined categories that identify specific segments, you can describe where attention is focused, based on aspects of the business that you can affect. Assessing how words are being used to describe these concepts can provide insight into the degree of attention. This kind of extraction provides details on specific features, offering much more detailed analysis. With more detailed insight, you can be more specific in defining priorities and any corresponding action.

For example, considering the tense of a verb can help identify a person's priorities or intention. The use of emotional words, including their frequency, can identify the degree to which someone cares.

Some describe this as using both the art and science – or the human and machine – aspects of analytics. An interesting thing is that with an integrated system, you have both. You can use your custom entities (human-defined) in your text mining (machine-learned). If the system is fully integrated, you can combine your structured and unstructured analysis simply by dragging and dropping a predictive model algorithm on discovered topics to see if they affect the likelihood of churn, for example.

Integration gives you choices in how to develop analytics and how you deploy the results. This kind of flexibility is vital to your operations as you become more responsive to your market, your different audiences and your different topics of investigation. To experience the many benefits that come from analysing social media, you need open, flexible and integrated analytic technology that can tell you how sentiment matters and in what context. Organizations leveraging the full benefits of sentiment analysis are improving results with performance benefits that go far beyond reputation management to cost savings and increased sales.

Employing AI in Business

Analytics Landscape

At the present time, great amounts of additional data will become available, including both structured data, such as from sensors, and unstructured data, such as from cameras, social media and sentiment from the social network. The main factor behind the growth of data-driven AI is the availability of vast amounts of data. This includes machine-generated data from new sources such as sensors or the so-called Internet of Things as well as human-generated data, both from within and outside the enterprise.

Business analytics is being used within the information technology industry to refer to the use of computing to gain insight from data. The data may be obtained from a company's internal sources, such as its enterprise resource planning application, data warehouses/marts, from a third-party data provider or from public sources. Companies seek to leverage the digitized data from transaction systems and automated business processes to support "fact-based" decision making. Thus, business analytics is a category of computing rather than a specific method, application or product.

Analytics is part of the evolution that can lead to successful AI system. Case in point, machine learning models are trained on huge data sets. In analytics-aware organization, that deal with data discovery, big data and tasks such as data wrangling, data preparation and integration, AI is a natural progression. A mature analytics system will underpin the success for AI. Another key area to consider is that AI systems mature over a period as they are fed more data and the right, quality data. Hence, businesses invest in data storage and data warehouse; this is part of the process of aligning assets for implementing AI.

Application Areas

Many functions within a business can benefit from analytics. The most common functional categories include:

(a) Customer Analytics: This category includes applications to marketing (customer profiling, segmentation, social network analysis, brand reputation analysis, marketing mix optimization) and customer experience. The *SNAzzy* (Social Network Analysis in Telecom) and *VOCA* (Voice-of-Customer- Analytics) technologies fall in this category.
(b) Supply Chain Analytics: This includes demand forecasting, and optimization of inventory, pricing, scheduling, transportation and storage, while mitigating and risk. IBM's optimization of its internal supply chain has produced impressive results. A subfield known as *Human Capital Analytics* aka *Workforce Analytics* applies to service industries where human resources are the main means of production.
(c) Fraud and Risk Analytics: This includes assessment of several types of risk (market, operational, credit) particularly in the Financial sector.
(d) Analytics in Public domain: Urged by natural resource constraints, governments are using analytics for tasks such as detecting water leakages in distribution systems, making energy grids and traffic systems smarter and improving public safety.

Complexity of Analytics

Complexity of analytics can be broken down into three layers: *Descriptive analytics* can be implemented using spreadsheets or industrial strength. *Predictive analytics* is about what will happen next, and *prescriptive analytics* is about how to achieve the best outcome. Business analytics focuses on five key areas of customer needs:

- *Information access:* This first segment is foundational to business analytics. It is all about fostering informed/collaborative decision making across the business – ensuring that decision makers can understand how their area of the business is doing so they can make informed decisions.
- *Insight:* Gaining a deeper understanding of why things are happening, for example, gaining a full view of your customer (transaction history, segmentation, sentiment and opinion, etc.) to make better decisions and enable profitable growth.
- *Foresight:* Leveraging the past to predict potential future outcomes so that actions and decisions are computed in order to meet the objectives and requirements of the business.
- *Business agility:* Driving real-time decision optimization in both people-centric and process/automated-centric processes.

- *Strategic alignment:* This segment of the market is about strategically aligning everyone in the business – from strategy to execution. It is about enabling enterprise and operational visibility. It is about documenting the preferences, priorities, objectives and requirements that drive decision making.

Organizations that undertake a journey into the applications of business analytics must begin with an information management agenda that treats data and information as a strategic asset. Once information is treated as an asset, then descriptive, predictive and prescriptive analytics can be applied. Classically, a business or an organization begins this journey by examining the data generated from its automation systems: enterprise resource planning, customer relationship management, time and attendance, e-commerce, warranty management and the like. The business may also have unstructured data, such as contracts, customer complaints, internal emails, and, increasingly, image data from facility monitoring systems, as well as unstructured data from various web sources, such as Facebook, Twitter and blogs. Together structured and unstructured data establishes a 360-degree view of information to improve decision making. Many of the business analytic techniques used for structured data can be applied to unstructured data as well (Akerkar 2013).

Descriptive Analytics

Most businesses start with descriptive analytics – the use of data to figure out what happened in the past. Descriptive analytics prepares and analyses historical data and identifies patterns from samples for reporting of trends. Techniques such as data modelling, visualization and regression analysis largely reside in this space.

It is a set of technologies and processes that use data to understand and analyse business performance.

Descriptive analytics can be classified into three areas that answer certain kinds of questions:

- *Standard reporting and dashboards:* What happened? How does it compare to our plan? What is happening now?
- Ad hoc *reporting:* How many? How often? Where?
- *Analysis/query/drill-down:* What exactly is the problem? Why is it happening?

Descriptive analytics are the most commonly used and most well-understood type of analytics. Descriptive analytics categorizes, characterizes, consolidates and classifies data. Descriptive analytics includes dashboards, reports (e.g. budget, sales, revenue, and costs) and diverse types of queries. Tools for descriptive analytics may provide mechanisms for interfacing to enterprise data sources. They typically include report generation, distribution capability and data visualization facilities. Descriptive analytics techniques are most commonly applied to structured data, although there have been numerous efforts to extend their reach to unstructured data, often through the creation of structured metadata and indices.

Descriptive analytics help provide an understanding of the past as well as events occurring in real time.

Many descriptive analytics applications are implemented through out-of-the-box business intelligence software solutions or spreadsheet tools; however, version control difficulties may result from a proliferation of spreadsheets. The advantage of a descriptive analytics software platform (business intelligence and information/data management software) is the connectivity it provides to the underlying trusted information management system, as well as the ability to work with data along multiple dimensions to gain insight. Insight into what is happening now or has happened in the past can be useful in making decisions about the future, but descriptive analytics relies on the human review of data and does not contain robust techniques that facilitate understanding what might happen in the future, nor does it provide the tools to suggest decisions of what should be done next.

Descriptive analytics does provide significant insight into business performance and enables users to better monitor and manage their business processes. Additionally, descriptive analytics often serves as a first step in the successful application of predictive or prescriptive analytics. Organizations that effectively use descriptive analytics typically have a single view of the past and can focus their attention on the present, rather than on reconciling different views of the past.

Predictive Analytics

Predictive analytics uses data to find out what could happen in the future. Naturally it is a more refined and higher-level usage of analytics. Predictive analytics predicts future probabilities and trends and finds relationships in data not clear with old-style analysis. Techniques such as data mining and predictive modelling reside in this space. In particular, predictive analytics, a category of structured data analysis, uses data and mathematical techniques to uncover explanatory and predictive models of business performance representing the inherit relationship between data inputs and outputs.

Predictive analytics uses the understanding of the past to make "predictions" about the future. Predictive analytics is applied both in real time to affect the operational process (real-time retention actions via chat messages or real-time identification of suspicious transactions) and in batch (target new customers on website or direct mail to drive cross-sell/up-sell, predict churn, etc.). These predictions are made by examining data about the past, detecting patterns or relationships in this data and then extrapolating these relationships forward in time. For example, an insurance claim that falls into a category (pattern) that has proven worrying in the past might be flagged for closer investigation.

Predictive analytics can be classified into six categories:

- *Data mining:* What data is correlated with other data?
- *Pattern recognition and alerts:* When should I take action to correct or adjust a process or piece of equipment?

- *Monte-Carlo simulation:* What could happen?
- *Forecasting:* What if these trends continue?
- *Root cause analysis:* Why did something happen?
- *Predictive modelling:* What will happen next?

Descriptive analytics may begin by providing a static view of the past, but as more instances are accumulated in the data sources that document past experience, the steps of evaluation, classification and categorization can be performed repetitively by fast algorithms, endowing the overall work process with a measure of adaptability. As descriptive analytics reach the stage where they support anticipatory action, a threshold is passed into the domain of predictive analytics. Predictive analytics applies advanced techniques to examine scenarios and helps to detect hidden patterns in massive quantities of data in order to project future events. It uses techniques that segment and group data (transaction, individuals, events, etc.) into coherent sets in order to predict behaviour and detect trends. It utilizes techniques such as clustering, expert rules, decision trees and neural networks. Predictive analytics is most commonly used to calculate potential behaviour in ways that allow one to:

- Examine time series, evaluating past data and trends to predict future demands (level, trend, seasonality). Advanced methods include identifying cyclical patterns, isolating the impact of external events (e.g., weather), characterizing inherent variability and detecting trends.
- Determine "causality" relationships between two or more time series, for example, forecasting the demand for replacement parts at a municipal bus maintenance facility by considering both historical usage rates and known, predicted or seasonal changes in passenger demand.
- Extract patterns from large data quantities via data mining, to predict nonlinear behaviour not easily identifiable through other approaches. This predicted behaviour can be used to create policies that automate actions to be taken in the future; for example, by classifying past insurance claims, future claims can be flagged for investigation if they have a high probability of being fraudulent. In operational terms, predictive analytics may be applied as a guide to answer questions such as:
  - Who are my best customers and what is the best way to target them?
  - Which patients are most likely to respond to a given treatment?
  - Is this insurance application likely to be rejected?
  - Is this a suspicious transaction that may be fraudulent?

It is at this level that the term "advanced analytics" is more aptly applied. Included are techniques for predictive modelling and simulation as well as forecasting. In simulation, a model of the system is created; estimates or predictions about the future behaviour of the system are made by exercising the model under a variety of scenarios. Simulation requires being able to build algorithms or mathematical constructs that provide a sufficiently accurate representation of the observable behaviour of a system. This in turn can be used to evaluate proposed changes to a system before they are implemented, thus minimizing cost and risk.

Much of business process modelling falls into this category. Forecasting, which is part of predictive analytics, can be applied in many ways, not the least of which is predicting workload, which is often translated into resources required, including human resources. The forecasting activity establishes a desired end state, and details are subsequently translated into an agreed upon operational plan (enter enterprise planning activity) and together descriptive, advanced analytics, enterprise planning and final mile close/consolidate/compliance activities form a closed-loop performance management system that repeats over and over again within an business.

Predictive modelling techniques can also be used to examine data to evaluate hypotheses. If each data point (or observation) is comprised of multiple attributes, then it may be useful to understand whether some combinations of a subset of attributes are predictive of a combination of other attributes. For example, one may examine insurance claims in order to validate the hypothesis that age, gender and zip code can predict the likelihood of an auto insurance claim. Predictive modelling tools can aid in both validating and generating hypotheses. This is particularly useful when some of the attributes are actions determined by the business decision makers.

Data is at the heart of predictive analytics, and to drive a complete view, data is combined from descriptive data (attributes, characteristics, geo/demographics), behaviour data (orders, transaction, payment history), interaction data (email, chat transcripts, web click-streams) and attitudinal data (opinions, preferences, needs and desires). With a full view, customers can achieve higher performance such as dramatically lowering costs of claims, fighting fraud and maximizing payback, turning a call centre into a profit centre, servicing customers faster and effectively reducing costs.

Beyond capturing the data, accessing trusted and social data inside and outside of the business, and modelling and applying predictive algorithms, deployment of the model is just as vital in order to maximize the impact of analytics in real-time operations.

Predictive analytics applications Predictive analytics can be used in many applications. Here we cite some examples where it has made a positive impact.

Medical decision support system Experts use predictive analytics in healthcare primarily to determine which patients are at risk of developing certain conditions like diabetes, asthma, heart disease and other lifetime illnesses.

Fraud detection Fraud is widely spread across industries. Cases of fraud appear in diverse fields such as credit card activations, invoices, tax returns, online activities, insurance claims and telecom call activities. All these industries are interested in detecting frauds and bringing those responsible to book and preventing and monitoring fraud at reasonable costs. Predictive modelling can help them achieve these objectives. The may also be used to detect financial statement fraud in companies.

Insurance Like fraud, unexpectedly high and suspicious claims are the bane of insurance companies. They would like to avoid paying such claims. Though the objective is simple enough, predictive modelling has had only partial success in eliminating this source of high loss to companies. This is a promising area of further research.

Health While the systematic applications of predictive modelling in healthcare are relatively new, the fundamental applications are similar to those in the other areas. After all minimizing customer risk is the objective. In healthcare this is the risk of readmission, which can be reduced by identifying high-risk patients and monitoring them.

Financial prediction Predictive analytics is useful in financial predictions.

Analytical customer relationship management (CRM) Analytical customer relationship management is a frequent commercial application of predictive analytics. CRM uses predictive analytics in applications for marketing campaigns, sales and customer services to name a few.

Customer retention By a frequent examination of a customer's past service usage, performance, spending and other behaviour patterns, predictive models can determine the likelihood of a customer wanting to terminate a service soon.

A wide variety of techniques can be used to build predictive analytic models:

- Neural networks can assess how likely it is that a credit card transaction is being performed by the cardholder by evaluating how close this transaction is to the patterns predicted by that person's past behaviour.
- Regression models can determine which characteristics of a customer make it more likely that they will churn, or attrite, enabling a calculation of the risk of future churn.
- Response models can predict how likely a particular person is to respond to a particular marketing offer, based on the success or failure of offers made in the past.
- Predictive scorecards can determine the likelihood that someone will fail to make payments on his or her loan in the coming year.

These predictions of risk, fraud and customer opportunity are all created from enormous amounts of historical data. To build these models, you need not just data, but data over time. Data changing over time reveals behaviour and patterns. As noted above, we have the most data for our operations. Therefore, our operational environment is where we have the data we need to build predictive analytic models.

Prescriptive Analytics

Prescriptive analytics uses data to prescribe the best course of action to increase the chances of realizing the best outcome. Prescriptive analytics evaluates and determines new ways to operate, targets business objectives and balances all constraints. Techniques such as optimization and simulation reside in this space. Businesses, as they strive to become more analytically mature, have indicated a goal to move up the analytics hierarchy to optimize their business or operational processes. They see the prescriptive use of analytics as a differentiating factor for their business that will allow them to break away from the competition. Clearly, analytics leads to optimization. But it is also clear that optimization is dependent on the analytics process. It is a set of mathematical techniques that computationally determine a set of high-value alternative actions or decisions given a complex set of objectives, requirements and constraints, with the goal of improving business performance.

Prescriptive analytics, which is part of "advanced analytics", is based on the concept of optimization, which can be divided into two areas:

- Optimization: How can we achieve the best outcome?
- Stochastic optimization: How can we achieve the best outcome and address uncertainty in the data to make better decisions?

Once the past is understood and predictions can be made about what might happen in the future, it is then time to think about what the best response or action will be, given the limited resources of the enterprise. This is the area of prescriptive analytics. Many problems simply involve too many choices or alternatives for a human decision maker to effectively consider, weigh and trade off – scheduling or work planning problems, for example. In the past, these problems could only be solved using computers running algorithms on a particular data set for hours or even days. It was not useful to embed such problem-solving capability into a decision support system since it could not provide timely results. Now, however, with improvements in the speed and memory size of computers, as well as the considerable progress in the performance of the underlying mathematical algorithms, similar computations can be performed in minutes. While this kind of information might have been used in the past to shape policy and offer guidance on action in a class of situations, assessments can now be completed in real time to support decisions to modify actions, assign resources and so on.

Embedding AI into Business Processes

The use of AI in business is rising, but AI and machine learning are not yet an effective use for every business operation. While there are many aspects of a business which can be automated, and should be automated, tasks that require judgement, prioritization and trade-offs still require human intelligence.

Embedding AI into specific business processes where it can produce positive results is a good place to start. Over time, it will become natural to integrate AI into any new business initiative. Ultimately, your business-wide AI proficiency should include:

- *Defining who will lead and be accountable for AI initiatives*
- *Identifying people in your business with AI expertise or going outside your business to recruit talent*
- *Determining where AI can add value or address pain points*
- *Using AI to enhance the capabilities that are most critical to business success*
- *Improving decision making and other processes with automated intelligence*

Actions that require computation or organizing copious quantities of data are all better handled by machines and applying automated solutions that use AI will wipe out other old-style business models. Businesses gather massive amounts of data from business operations, social interactions and sensors. Utilizing the power of big data to build automated solutions and provide insights will lead to sustainable competitive advantage.

It is reasonable that the distinction may become blurred, especially as AI technologies advance. To determine the best strategy, businesses should question whether the task at hand allows for repetition, high volume, a pattern and low cost of mistakes. The tasks that satisfy these specific criteria are starting points for AI implementation.

AI can be used to provide better responses to transaction requests by proficiently collecting historical chat data. Processes at the edge of business, in which the cost of making mistakes is low, is also a right opportunity to apply AI.

Once a business regulates which tasks can be automated, it can establish how AI can be successfully implemented. To accomplish this, businesses should reference the following checklist:

- *Recognize the problem*
  - Begin by recognizing the business problem and ask where using AI can improve efficiency.
- *Identify the data source*
  - Once the problem is identified, distinguish the data source and collect data from relevant customer touch points.
- *Develop an AI-based solution*
  - Develop an AI-based solution to aid algorithmic decision making and make use of neural networks and NLP.

Implementation and Action

Subsequently, an AI solution can be recurrently implemented. Training should follow for staff to effectively work with AI and understand its use and applications for appropriate situations, as well as provide human intervention when necessary. By illuminating the implementation process, businesses can set genuine expectations on just how AI will begin to affect their business, while taking advantage of what the technology could offer.

Finally, remember that the goal of any new product, service or experience is to provide the best solution for your customer. Avoid taking a technology-first approach that prefers the technology over their needs and use modern technology to provide for the needs that you identified earlier. Technology works best when it is invisible and works in the background. Artificial intelligence is no different. People should never know that they are dealing with AI. They should feel that they are being served well by the company they have chosen to provide them with the product, service or experience.

Like any technology, applied AI is really nothing more than a tool that businesses use to accomplish a task. Its value lies in how well it does this. Eventually, this means its value is measured in how well companies use it to serve their customers well. Once the innovation of artificial intelligence wears off, this is really all that will be left. So, to unlock the value of AI, it is best to move past the technology completely and serve your customers well.

Artificial Intelligence for Growth

AI for Customer Service

Nowadays, customers are tied to their devices all the time and switch between them impeccably. There is a growing rift between the amount of customer data being generated and the capacity for traditional marketing techniques – largely powered by human analysis – to process this data. Advances in big data technologies like Hadoop have made it easy to capture raw data in diverse formats and store them across several different data stores usually called data lakes spanning SQL systems, NoSQL systems, flat files and excel sheets. This is the raw gold mine you are working with and you should prioritize data capture in any format over shoehorning it to a data store or schema. AI tools that you invest in should adapt to this mix of structured and unstructured data.

The half-life of consumer intent is getting shorter with each passing year, and customers expect "on-demand" experiences that are contextually relevant and personalized to them across every device. Growth marketers should prioritize simpler AI algorithms and processes that can adapt well to real-time data than more complex batch mode solutions that may need several hours or days to execute. Pay close attention to training time it takes to build and deploy AI models and how fast can they incorporate new data.

While it is ideal to have every attribute and preference known about all users, you will end up with incomplete or partially known data fields despite your best efforts. B2C growth marketers in particular should expect this from day one and invest in tools and solutions that adapt well to incomplete data. Take for example a user location, there may be a mix of user given location data, with device latitude/longitude, IP to geo, inferences from content viewed or searches done and more. As a growth marketer you should prefer AI tools that can adapt well to the mix of all this data and output best effort answers for widest user base than on few users with complete and clean data.

Several AI algorithms expect training data to be fed to them and the size and availability of training data is big obstacle to overcome to use them effectively. Certain class of AI algorithms like Boosted Random Forests are better at adapting to the size of training data than convolutional neural networks a kind of deep learning. Growth marketers should prefer those algorithms that can work with limited training data and have in-built sampling techniques to deal with disproportionate class sizes.

Effective use of AI can narrow this human cognitive challenge by processing these large volumes of data quickly and use machine learning to recognize patterns in the data and predict what to do next based on the past behaviour of similar audiences. While this sounds logical and straightforward, it is not as easy as buying a black-box AI system and dropping it in.

The decision to deploy an AI system to improve marketing performance is a big one that should be given the same level of planning and preparation that was given to deploying a system or your marketing automation system. The AI powered system will become your system of intelligence that must work closely with these other systems to improve results.

Applying AI for Marketing

In marketing, data unification is their greatest challenge when they want to make the most of their customer data. Having existing data silos is one of the main reasons why marketers cannot fully leverage all their customer data. With AI, however, marketers can successfully break data silos and effectively generate and orchestrate customer insights and actionable intelligence.

Many businesses aspire to become customer-centric and data-driven, yet few can turn data into profitable actions. AI can link this gap and enable marketers to become customer-led, insights-driven, fast and connected. AI will give them greater visibility into customer behaviour, make appropriate and contextual offers and deliver personalized and unified experiences across all channels. And based on the insights generated, AI empowers marketers to further optimize their offerings and overall strategy.

AI adoption impacts not just marketing processes but the entire business. Determine the organizational gaps that must be closed and address the factors and fallacies that may hinder the business from implementing AI. It is necessary to draw out the customer journey and include all steps in the process beyond just what happens in marketing. Understand where the bottlenecks are and address the key pieces that you wish to have AI help you solve. Further, it is important to ensure that everyone in the business has the right understanding of AI. For instance, they should be aware that AI alone cannot convey knowledge. It requires both people and technology. Which brings us to the next step.

Marketers should know how to deploy AI effectively and set the right controls and monitoring systems. Should they turn on a model and let it generate results for people to review? Or, should they embed it into an application that automates processes such as personalizing content and optimizing email campaigns? How will they put the right controls and monitoring to ensure that models are working properly and delivering results?

Empowering AI-powered marketing can result in an optimized customer journey, greater efficiency, smarter decisions, increased speed and continuous performance improvement.

Businesses adopting AI expect to see increased productivity. New competences can be derived from streamlining tasks that hitherto took people days to complete and improving work processes by pairing people and machines in new ways. Many businesses also believe AI will accelerate and enhance innovation, further creating new jobs. Some expect to see amplified consumer demand from more personalized and higher-quality AI-enhanced products and services. At the same time, some worry that AI will result in eliminating jobs. But to capitalize on the technology, businesses will need to hire people with AI experience or the skills to analyze and use the data. Businesses also need the computing power and system infrastructure to support AI-enabled products and services, and they need platforms to organize and integrate their data. Getting this infrastructure in place can be expensive. The data collected by AI offers another big challenge. How do businesses guarantee it is valid? What limits do they need to put on its use? Can safeguards confirm that machines carry out human orders as intended? There are concerns that unintentional biases may find their way into AI algorithms or decision-making models. Businesses need to establish robust controls to prevent this from happening and monitor the systems that learn through AI. Letting stakeholders know about the business's oversight can help establish trust with stakeholders that businesses are using AI reliably.

Glossary

A

Algorithms A formula or set of rules for performing a task. In AI, the algorithm tells the machine how to go about finding answers to a question or solutions to a problem.

Artificial intelligence A machine's ability to make decisions and perform tasks that simulate human intelligence and behaviour.

Artificial neural network (ANN) A learning model created to act like a human brain that solves tasks that are too difficult for traditional computer systems to solve.

Autonomic computing A system's capacity for adaptive self-management of its own resources for high-level computing functions without user input.

Analogical reasoning Solving problems by using analogies, by comparing to past experiences.

Autonomous Autonomy is the ability to act independently of a ruling body. In AI, a machine or vehicle is referred to as autonomous if it does not require input from a human operator to function properly.

B

Backpropagation Backpropagation is a way of training neural networks based on a known, desired output for specific sample case.

Backward chaining A method in which machines work backward from the desired goal, or output, to determine if there is any data or evidence to support those goals or outputs.

Big data Big data is datasets that are so voluminous and complex that traditional data processing application software is inadequate to deal with them.

C

Case-based reasoning (CBR) An approach to knowledge-based problem solving that uses the solutions of a past, similar problem (case) to solve an existing problem.

Chatbots A chat robot (chatbot for short) that is designed to simulate a conversation with human users by communicating through text chats, voice commands, or both. They are a commonly used interface for computer programs that include AI capabilities.

Classification Classification algorithms let machines assign a category to a data point based on training data. All the examples in the training set must be labelled by humans before the system can be trained. In image classification, for example, the inputs are digital images, and the labels are the names of various objects that appear in these images ("cat", "car", "person", etc.). To train a classifier, we need to not only label our data, but first define the set of labels we will use. The examples for different labels need to be distinguishable, and each label must have a reasonable number of example occurrences in our training set. Classifier training generally works best if the different labels are roughly "balanced", that is, all have roughly the same number of examples. Popular machine learning systems for classification include neural networks, support vector machines, and random forests.

Cluster analysis A type of unsupervised learning used for exploratory data analysis to find hidden patterns or grouping in data; clusters are modelled with a measure of similarity defined by metrics such as Euclidean or probabilistic distance.

Clustering Clustering algorithms let machines group data points or items into groups with similar characteristics.

Cognitive computing A computerized model that mimics the way the human brain thinks. It involves self-learning through the use of data mining, natural language processing, and pattern recognition.

Convolutional neural network (CNN) A special neural network architecture especially useful for processing image and speech data. The difference between a normal feed-forward network and a convolutional network is primarily in the mathematical processing that takes place. Convolutional networks use an operation known as convolution to help correlate features of their input across space or time, making them good at picking out complex, extended features. However, they still treat each input separately, without a memory.

D

Data mining The examination of data sets to discover and mine patterns from that data that can be of further use.

Data science An interdisciplinary field that combines scientific methods, systems, and processes from statistics, information science, and computer science to provide insight into phenomenon via either structured or unstructured data.

Decision tree A tree and branch-based model used to map decisions and their possible consequences, similar to a flow chart.

Deep learning Deep learning is a type of machine learning in artificial intelligence. It utilizes multiple levels of artificial neural networks to solve problems. The artificial neural networks are built like the human brain, with nodes connected together like a web. While programs analyse data linearly, deep learning enables machines to process data nonlinearly by passing on data from one node to the next, which, after each pass improves the machine's accuracy. Deep learning is generally used for high-scale, complex problems.

F

Feature (feature selection, feature learning) A variable that is used as an input to a model.

Feature learning An ensemble of techniques meant to automatically discover the representations needed for feature detection or classification from raw data.

Forward chaining A situation where an AI system must work "forward" from a problem to find a solution. Using a rule-based system, the AI would determine which "if" rules it would apply to the problem.

G

Game AI A form of AI specific to gaming that uses an algorithm to replace randomness. It is a computational behaviour used in non-player characters to generate human-like intelligence and reaction-based actions taken by the player.

General Data Protection Regulation (GDPR) A regulation in EU law on data protection and privacy for all individuals within the European Union aiming to give control to citizens and residents over their personal data.

Genetic algorithm An evolutionary algorithm based on principles of genetics and natural selection that is used to find optimal or near-optimal solutions to difficult problems that would otherwise take decades to solve.

H

Heuristic search techniques Support that narrows down the search for optimal solutions for a problem by eliminating options that are incorrect.

Heuristics These are rules drawn from experience used to solve a problem more quickly than traditional problem-solving methods in AI. While faster, a heuristic approach typically is less optimal than the classic methods it replaces.

I

Image segmentation The term image segmentation refers to the partition of an image into a set of regions that cover it. The goal in many tasks is for the regions to represent meaningful areas of the image, such as the crops, urban areas, and forests of a satellite image.

Inductive reasoning In AI, inductive reasoning uses evidence and data to create statements and rules.

Intelligence Intelligence can be defined in many different ways including someone's capacity for logic, understanding, self-awareness, learning, emotional knowledge, planning, creativity, and problem solving. Artificial intelligence is intelligence displayed by machines, in contrast to the natural intelligence displayed by humans and other animals.

K

Knowledge engineering Focuses on building knowledge-based systems, including all of the scientific, technical, and social aspects of it.

L

Layer (hidden layer) A series of neurons in an artificial neural network that process a set of input features, or, by extension, the output of those neurons.

Logic programming A type of programming paradigm in which computation is carried out based on the knowledge repository of facts and rules; LISP and Prolog are two logic programming languages used for AI programming.

M

Machine intelligence An umbrella term that encompasses machine learning, deep learning, and classical learning algorithms.

Machine learning A facet of AI that focuses on algorithms, allowing machines to learn without being programmed and change when exposed to new data.

Machine perception The ability for a system to receive and interpret data from the outside world similarly to how humans use our senses. This is typically done with attached hardware, though software is also usable.

N

Natural language processing The ability for a program to recognize human communication as it is meant to be understood.

O

Ontology/ontologies In the context of information science, an ontology is a formal set of definitions, properties, or relationships between entities of a particular knowledge domain. Ontologies are useful in different scientific domains to categorize or classify terms.

P

Planning A branch of AI dealing with planned sequences or strategies to be performed by an AI-powered machine. Things such as actions to take, variable to account for, and duration of performance are accounted for.

Pruning The use of a search algorithm to cut off undesirable solutions to a problem in an AI system. It reduces the number of decisions that can be made by the AI system.

Pattern recognition An area of machine learning focusing on the (supervised or unsupervised) recognition of patterns in the data.
Precision The number of correct positive results divided by the number of all positive results returned by a classifier.
Prediction The inferred output of a trained model provided with an input instance.
Preprocessing The process of transforming raw data into a more understandable format.
Pre-trained model A model, or the component of a model, that have been preliminary trained, generally using another data set. See also: Transfer Learning.
Prior The probability distribution that would represent the pre-existing beliefs about a specific quantity before new evidence is considered.

R
Random forest An ensemble learning method that operates by constructing a multitude of decision trees at training time and outputting a combined version (such as the mean or the mode) of the results of each individual tree.
Recurrent neural network (RNN) A type of neural network that makes sense of sequential information and recognizes patterns, and creates outputs based on those calculations.
Reinforcement learning Reinforcement learning is a form of machine learning where the system interacts with a changing, dynamic environment and is presented with (positive and negative) feedback as it takes actions in response to this environment. There is no predefined notion of a "correct" response to a given stimulus, but there are notions of "better" or "worse" ones that can be specified mathematically in some way. Reinforcement learning is often used to train machine learning systems to play video games, or drive cars.

S
Semantic segmentation A complex form of image segmentation that involves labelling every single pixel in an image with one of potentially hundreds of category labels describing what kind of object the pixel is a part of.
Supervised learning A type of machine learning in which output datasets train the machine to generate the desired algorithms, like a teacher supervising a student; more common than unsupervised learning.
Swarm behaviour From the perspective of the mathematical modeller, it is an emergent behaviour arising from simple rules that are followed by individuals and does not involve any central coordination.
Sentiment analysis Sentiment analysis involves taking variably sized chunks of human-generated text as inputs, and automatically determining whether the views being expressed are overall positive, negative, or neutral. This can be a very subjective and context-specific task, but also one of immediate value to advertisers and marketers. Beyond positive/negative/neutral, other forms of sentiment analysis can involve classifying text as objective vs. subjective, or attempting to classify the emotional state of the author in more detail.

T

Turing test A test developed by Alan Turing that tests the ability of a machine to mimic human behaviour. The test involves a human evaluator who undertakes natural language conversations with another human and a machine and rates the conversations.

U

Uncertainty A range of values likely to enclose the true value.

Underfitting The fact that a machine learning algorithm fails to capture the underlying structure of the data properly, typically because the model is either not sophisticated enough, or not appropriate for the task at hand; opposite of Overfitting.

Unsupervised learning A type of machine learning algorithm used to draw inferences from datasets consisting of input data without labelled responses. The most common unsupervised learning method is cluster analysis.

References

Akerkar, R. (Ed.). (2013). *Big Data Computing*. New York: Chapman and Hall/CRC.
Akerkar, R., & Lingras, P. (2008). *Building an intelligent web: Theory and practice*. Sudbury: Jones & Bartlett.
Akerkar, R. A., & Sajja, P. S. (2010). *Knowledge based systems*. Sudbury: Jones & Bartlett.
Arel, I., Rose, D., & Coop, R. (2009). DeSTIN: A scalable deep learning architecture with application to high-dimensional robust pattern recognition. AAAI Fall Symposium (pp. 11–15), Washington.
Arel, I., Rose, D. C., & Karnowski, T. P. (2010). Deep machine learning-a new frontier in artificial intelligence research. *Computational Intelligence Magazine, IEEE, 5*(4), 13–18.
Ash, T. (1989). Dynamic node creation in backpropagation neural networks. *Connection Science, 1*(4), 365–375.
Bengio, Y., Courville, A., & Vincent, P. (2013). Representation learning: A review and new perspectives. *IEEE Transactions on Pattern Analysis and Machine Intelligence, 35*(8), 1798–1828.
Davenport, T. H., & Harris, J. G. (2007). *Competing on analytics: the new science of winning* (p. 7). Boston, Mass: Harvard Business School.
Malhotra, K. N., & Birks, F. D. (2000). *Marketing research. An applied approach* (European ed.). London: Pearson.
Ricci, F., Rokach, L., Shapira, B., & Kantor, P. B. (2011). *Recommender systems handbook* (1st ed.). US: Springer.
Thomas M. Mitchell. 1997. Machine learning (1st ed.). McGraw-Hill, Inc., New York.
Tuk, M. (2012). Cluster analysis, marketing analytics. Imperial College London, unpublished.

GPSR Compliance

The European Union's (EU) General Product Safety Regulation (GPSR) is a set of rules that requires consumer products to be safe and our obligations to ensure this.

If you have any concerns about our products, you can contact us on

ProductSafety@springernature.com

In case Publisher is established outside the EU, the EU authorized representative is:

Springer Nature Customer Service Center GmbH
Europaplatz 3
69115 Heidelberg, Germany

www.ingramcontent.com/pod-product-compliance
Ingram Content Group UK Ltd.
Pitfield, Milton Keynes, MK11 3LW, UK
UKHW022121230426
12048UKWH00010BA/638